Cover: FAREWELL TO ANGER Palette Knife by Leonid Afremov

Healthy Parts

Happy Self

3 Steps to Like Yourself

By Gordon Emmerson

Copyright 2012 Gordon Emmerson

ISBN-13:

978-1481006729

ISBN-10:

148100672X

*****

> *I am my parts*
>
> *I know my parts*
>
> *I know myself*

The notion that we are made up of different parts, rather than just having a single part with different moods, is exciting and challenging. Each of our parts has its own traits and skills. Our language indicates that we already know this. We have phrases like, "Part of me wants to do that, but part of me does not," or "Part of me loves her, and part of me never wants to see her again."

This book is about our parts. You are in a part right now, reading it. Just as the sections in the book will change, the state you are in will change as you read. Right now you may be in a part that is excited about what you might find, and you may have another part that is cautious. It is good to have a variety of parts to help us. You will become able to recognize your different parts and you will learn to use them to your advantage.

Table of Contents

Unit 1: How things are 9

    Chapter 1: Discovering our Parts..9

    Chapter 2: Becoming Free 13

    Chapter 3: What is inside us..19

    Chapter 4: Healthy, Normal Resource States 39

Unit 2: How to Change 46

    Chapter 5: Healing the Vaded State 46

    Chapter 6: Making sure we have the right Resource State out 58

    Chapter 7: Achieving respect among our states, Peace Within...65

Unit 3: What can be changed?...76

    Chapter 8: Weight 76

    Chapter 9: Sleep 95

    Chapter 10: Competition 112

    Chapter 11: Addictions 117

    Addictions: Drug addiction 118

        Addictions: Gambling..130

        Addictions: Obsessive Compulsive Disorder................137

        Addictions: Compulsive spending.................................144

    Chapter 12: Depression..148

    Chapter 13: Anger 153

    Chapter 14: Grieving 171

Chapter 15: Self esteem 177
Chapter 16: Moving from mean behaviour to caring behaviour 189
Chapter 17: Communication and the way we respond to others 194
Chapter 18: Health 203
Chapter 19: Honesty 211
Chapter 20: Sex 223
Chapter 21: Meet some of your states 233
Chapter 22: Enjoyment 243
Chapter 23: Other than Resource States what else is inside? 252
Chapter 24: Growth and being ready for it 276
Chapter 25: Putting it all together 288

Poems [1]

A Thousand Years 15
The Roughened Shell 73
Spring 176
Love 236
Dreams 241
Fly Ride the Storm 292

All poems in this text were written by the author.

Three steps to Happiness

A prayer to ourselves should be, "Let me be me. Don't compel me to do or be something else."

There are three things our parts need so we can be happy being who we are. Here they are and here is how this book will guide you to get there.

1. We need the right part out at the right time. Our parts, our Resource States, are our resources and we need to have the best one out for the occasion all the time. Here are some examples, and you will learn in this book how to make sure you get the right part out.

Getting a hug from a loved one: You need a fragile part out that can enjoy the hug. No use being in an intellectual or business state.

Being criticized: You need an emotionless intellectual part out that can hear what is being said without feeling cut. A brain part will be able to rationally assess what is being said and respond from the head, not from the gut.

2. All of our parts need to like each other. Sometimes we have parts that don't like other parts. We may even say, "I hate that part of myself, I wish I did not have that lazy part," or, "I don't know why I do those things." We can feel like we are at war with ourselves, or that we are in to fight against ourselves to get what we want. Our Resource States need to learn the value of each other, how to get along, and how to compromise.

3. Our inner injuries need to heal. We have tender places inside, injured Resource States that feel upset when they come out. When they come out we often are not able to respond the way we would like. We may feel defensive, competitive, angry, anxious, or even unlovable. We may try to escape into an addiction, into food or shopping. These Resource States need to be able to feel empowered and supported so we can be in control, and so we can be who we really are.

This book is written in three sections. The first section describes **how things are**. In this section we learn what is on the inside. It is amazing how we are made up and when we discover our parts we understand ourselves.

The second section is about **how to change**. Here we learn exactly what to do to have the right part out, to have peace between our parts, and we learn how to heal injured parts.

The third section gives point by point illustrations for **making changes** in your life relating to specific issues, like weight control, sleep problems, addictions, self-esteem, and many others.

Writer's note: The training in this book may help many find real and lasting changes, but no book is a therapist. A therapist is able to respond individually to the needs of a client. Use this book to gain a higher level of internal peace and mental health, and at the same time be aware that good therapists are available.

Unit 1: How things are

Chapter 1: Discovering our Parts

It is amazing that we spend so much time focusing on the outside without becoming aware of the inside.

It is good that we have different Resource States. They help us do and enjoy different things. Some of our states have very little emotion, and are good at thinking, or doing mental problems. Others are very emotional. Some are happy to do mindless tasks, and others are bored by them. Some are able to feel love, and others have different roles.

What we experience as confusion is actually our parts wanting different things. When our parts do not recognize and respect each other we feel confused and sometimes out of control, "I did not want to eat that, but when that part takes over I lose control."

It is not good to hear an argument in our head that brings us stress, but it is good to be able to hear our different parts when they respect each other and when they are able to work together. If we consider buying a new car we want to hear from the part that wants to enjoy the car, and from the part that understands the budget. We may feel ourselves going back and forth in a decision as we switch between our parts, "This is so beautiful, look at that interior,"... "What am I doing here? I can't afford this. There are other things I need more."... "But I could cut back a little here and there and make it work, and it is so nice."

So, it is good for our parts to use each other to make good decisions, but it is not good if our different Resource States dislike, or hate each other. That gives us a feeling of inner conflict. The good thing is that we can bring peace to what is inside us.

Benefits to Learning about our Resource States

When we learn about our states we learn about ourselves. We know the parts of us and know who we are. We can become empowered to be who we want to be, and we can learn how our parts can make peace with each other so we can feel better in our skin. Here are just a few benefits to learning about our states and to helping them get what they need.

> **If we have the wrong state out we feel uncomfortable in our skin.**

Having the right state out at the right time

Our Resource States are our inner resources. Some states are excellent at doing specific things and it is good if we learn to have the right state out at the right time. When we have the wrong state out we feel uncomfortable in our skin. If I am going to study I want to be in a state that is interested in the topic and wants to learn about it. I don't want to be in a state that wants to be out playing in the sun. If I am taking a test after studying I want to be in the same state that studied so I will have the best recall, and I don't want to be in a nervous state that may not remember a lot of what the study part of me learned. There are hundreds of examples of this, but we have states that are better at communication, at sports, or at figuring things out. Why not learn to have the right state out at the right time?

Experiencing inner peace

When our states learn to respect and appreciate each other we don't get the arguments in our heads. We don't dislike parts of ourselves. Our self-concept improves and we feel more internally integrated.

Healing the tender spots in our psyche

There is one more big reason to learn about our parts. We each have parts that have taken on some fear or insecurity that we are still holding. When we have a Resource State that is carrying something upsetting from the past, that part can come out and give us that bad feeling today, causing us to feel out of control and to feel or act in a way that we don't want. We may feel really scared when we try to talk to a group. We may feel little and abused when someone talks to us in a demanding way. We may have difficulty controlling our anger. We may have a fear that we will fail and this fear can keep us from living in the way we would really like to live. We may have a need to compete that compels us to do things that we really are not interested in doing, or it may compel us to buy things that we really don't want.

When these parts from our past that carry upset feelings are able to feel empowered, safe and nurtured on the inside then we are free to be who we really are, free to do what we want to do. We no longer have to react out of fear or a need to please, but we can be our natural selves with an ability to react in ways that feel right for us.

Chapter 2: Becoming Free

What is being free?

For many being free feels so distant it cannot at first clearly be seen.

Being free is having the easy ability to be whoever we are. It is knowing who we are. It is having the courage to speak our beliefs. It is being able to love and be loved and know that what we present to the world is the real me; therefore when another person loves us we know it is really 'me' who is loved.

It is having the ability to answer the questions:

What is it 'I' really want?

We are often so lost in competition that we try to get something just because someone else has it, or so we can impress someone else. We may feel so insecure about who we are that we just want to look okay in other's eyes, so we set our sights on gaining what we think will help us feel okay, feel as good, or feel better. We may even fear the disapproval of others so much that we

> **Being free is having the easy ability to be whoever we are.**

attempt to buy or achieve things that we believe will best save us from their disapproval.

What would it be like to be able to focus free of others' demands, to be free to be ourselves? That does not mean that we will not consider others in our decisions, because considering the impact of our actions on those we care about is an important part of deciding what we most want. But there is a difference between making decisions out of fear or out of an understanding of what is right for us. A decision made from fear feels pressured while a decision made from understanding feels empowered.

Who am I?

In order to know what we want we need to know who we are. It is possible to have spent so much time trying to be what we think others want us to be that we have not had enough time to know who we really are. It may actually seem that a real person does not even exist. I believe that the most important part of living is knowing who we are and being able to share that with others. What is more meaningful than sharing honest feelings?

A Thousand Years

A thousand years from now what I have done, and what I do, will long have been forgotten.

The words I speak and paths I walk, will long be changed by thousands others' tongues and feet.

And even if reality is wed with plans inside my neighbor's head, the ruins will, by then, be rottened.

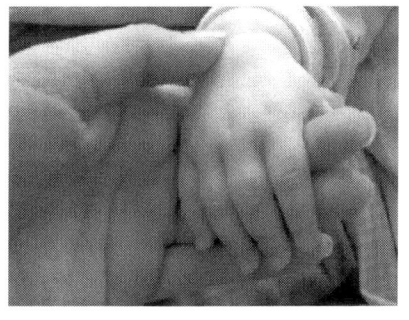

A thousand years from now what I have done, and do, may be lost in memory and meaning.

But not for now, and not for you, for now I'm filled with thoughts and feeling, as real to life, a thousand years from now, or hence, as any meaning.

Being real with our feelings allows us to experience the real moments of living. Being able to be who we really are, to show it and to live it removes the veil of fakeness and exposes us to the amazing life around us. It is a gift to others to show them the real person. It feels great when we feel that level of openness and honesty. We can have more of those 'being free' moments?

We are in lives worth living

The time that we are here is brief, and the world that we are in is filled with dynamic personalities, extraordinary physical features, and positive sensualities.

For life to be truly lived it is necessary for the psyche to be free. When we carry anger, resentment, jealousy, insecurity, and unresolved tender places in our psyches we are less than open and less than free.

Amazement, happiness, love, a loving kind of sadness and sorrow, fleeting anger, and appreciation, are flowing, living emotions. They are present in the light soul, and they are part of our interaction in this life.

Choosing Openness

To be open to the life about us we need to understand ourselves, we need to be psychologically healthy, and we need to have a philosophy that allows us to look at others with care or

It is right to fear a wild dog that might attack, but not to fear a disdainful look coming from a person whose life fails short of building positive interactions

sadness, without judgment or disdain.

Negativity is a dark heaviness that interferes with our ability to experience the world. It holds us down and back, and while we may think it is the fault of the person upon which we focus it, it is truly something we own, and we own it alone. If others have done us a disservice we continue to empower them and their disservice by allowing our lives to be restricted. Becoming free is severing that negative part of the connection mentally and emotionally.

Fears

It is right to fear a wild dog that might attack, but not to fear a disdainful look coming from a person whose life falls short of building positive interactions. These people may deserve from us avoidance, assertiveness, or help, but their inappropriate actions ought not to produce fear in a healthy personality. Healing our internal tender spots allows us to see them as they are, and frees us to react to them in the way we choose.

What energizes us

Being energized by what we want, rather than by a need to compete, frees us to know ourselves and be known by others. What better gift could we give ourselves and those about us than to reach the end of our lives and be able to say, '*I lived the real me!*'

Knowing, healing, and accepting our inner parts, our Resource States, is our path to freedom.

Chapter 3: What is inside us

It is extremely important to know our Resource States

Our parts

To become aware of the Resource States we have and to become aware of how they are feeling is like turning the lights on inside our own personality. We can finally see what is going on in there.

It is fascinating how we can change from one part to another and our whole outlook of living changes. We can switch from liking a person to not liking that person in an instant when we change from one part to another. We also can change from feeling light and happy to feeling heavy and sullen, and then back again to everything being okay.

> **We are always in one of our Resource States**

We are always in one of our Resource States, and we switch to another one very often. We might stay in a part from a few seconds to a few hours. When we switch from a part to a different part our feelings change, both how we feel about ourselves and how we feel about others. When we switch states, our abilities change. Our different parts have different skills, and sometimes we are not using the best part at the best time.

Think about being little. Your feet do not touch the floor. Your legs swing back and forth. Being little, with your legs swinging back and forth, think of another child saying this to you:

Sssh! Be really quiet. Don't turn your head. I don't want anyone else to hear this. I have a secret for you. It's a good one. No one is watching. The secret is, it is OK for us to be silly now, cause this is a really safe place.

Now, I want you to switch. I want to talk with a bigger 'thinking part' of you that considers ideas:

I want you to think about how long it may take you to finish this book. Do you want to read it? Time is important. Will this be time well spent? Do you want to learn about yourself, about your inner resources?

Did you feel the shift? The paragraph above with big letters was written to a child part of you that likes secrets. You may have felt a bit playful and maybe even a bit young. The second paragraph was written to a head part that thinks about things in order to figure them out. It may have had less feeling, and more intellect. Both are very important parts of you.

Here are some questions with answers that may help explain our parts. All the questions are written first.

How do our feelings change when we change Resource States?

Where did our Resource States come from and do all people have the same ones?

How many Resource States do we have?

Can we get new parts?

What happens if a part experiences something scary?

How can we learn to bring out the part we want out, when we want it out?

What do our parts need for us to be at peace and happy?

How do our feelings change when we change states?

Any time we are conscious we are in a Resource State. We have states that are not conscious, and these states that are not conscious at any given time are called our subconscious. They can hold memories that the conscious state does not remember, but when they come out they bring their memories out with them.

Sometimes we can feel a fast change of Resource States. We may be in a light hearted, fun loving Resource State and when we are asked to do a math problem we can switch states, feel more in the head, and then we can work on the problem. Then we may be able to return to the fun loving state again. The phrase, "I was in a good mood until you said that," is also saying, "I was in a light hearted Resource State until you said what you did, and now my ego is in a state that is more reactive or upset." The ego has changed states.

We have all learned how to bring states out for special purposes. The weight lifter learns to switch into a state that can focus and clear the mind, before lifting weights. When lifting weights the weight lifter is not in a state that is consciously considering which laundry detergent would be the best one to buy.

The lecturer, while lecturing, is not in a meditative, quiet state, and the chess player, while playing chess, is not in an amorous state, at least not normally.

We may find ourselves feeling uncomfortable in the state we are in. Some people go into a frightened state while speaking to a group and some may go into a state that spends money gambling, when other states don't want that to happen. It is possible to gain control of our Resource States. We will learn that in order to gain control and have the right state out, it does not take an internal struggle. It takes internal understanding.

Where did our Resource States come from and do we all have the same ones?

> **By repeating actions over and over again the brain will grow and connect in such a way that will create a physical neural pathway that is a Resource State**

We are not born with our different parts or Resource States. We make them as we live. Our parts are formed when we do something over and over again. This 'over and over again' learning creates a physical neural pathway in the brain that has its own level of emotion, abilities, and experience of living.

If, as a child, I bring my mother a cup of tea and she gives me a hug and thanks me, then the next time I want some nurturing I may do something nice for my mother or for someone else. If this continues to work for me, and I continue to do nurturing things for people, and I continue to get positive feedback, I will develop a nurturing Resource State. At future times in life, when I want to feel a connection with someone this nurturing part may come out and my feelings and actions will be nurturing. Some people may be good at bringing that part of me out.

If, as a child, I am feeling a need for attention and I tell a joke or do something funny, and if I get a positive response (that's really good, Gordon), and if I continue to get a positive response over months and years for being funny, I may develop a joking, comedian, Resource State. On the other hand, when I tell those first jokes, if I get a, "Be quiet Gordon" response, I will probably not develop a joking Resource State.

We each have our own special parts according to the experiences we have lived. The ways our family and friends react to us help us develop the particular Resource States we have.

By repeating actions over and over again the brain will grow and connect in such a way that will create a physical neural pathway that is a Resource State. We switch into a Resource State when a need for that state occurs, or when an injured state is reminded of the injury and comes out in an attempt to gain some resolution. That is why a bad feeling can come over us all at once.

Our brains are composed of cells, called neurons. We are born with most of the neurons we will ever have. We can lose them, and we can make more but it takes a lot of practice. Thankfully, we have a lot, and the ones we have can be trained, and retrained. While we do not easily grow new neurons we more easily grow new connections between our neurons. This is mainly how our brains grow, becoming bigger and heavier.

An interesting thing is that our brains grow according to stimulation. When mice were raised in an active environment their brains grew bigger than mice grown in a passive environment. Like muscles, brains grow bigger with use.

When kittens wore special goggles that allowed them to see only horizontal shapes for their first 4 or 5 months of life, they became mostly blind to vertical shapes when the goggles were removed. So our brains actually grow according to the amount of stimulation we get, and according to the type of stimulation we get. The goggles made the kittens practise seeing only horizontal shapes. When we do a nurturing behaviour over and over again, that is like the kittens' special goggles. Our brains develop according to that repeated nurturing behaviour.

That is how we develop Resource States. By doing the same type of activity over and over we grow connections that create a specific neural pathway that is a Resource State. Therefore, a Resource State is a physical part of our brain. Our brains are trained to have the Resource States we have. A Resource State is a grouping of neural fibres and connections that have been trained in such a way to provide us with specific skills.

Each of us has our own distinctive set of Resource States that we have trained. No one else will have Resource States that exactly match our own, but they may have some Resource States that are very similar to some of ours. When you meet someone who you feel comfortable with, you have met someone whose set of Resource States communicates well with yours. This is not to say that their Resource States are necessarily similar to yours. Some people say opposites attract, but when we meet people who have Resource States similar to ours we can feel like we have a natural understanding of them.

How many Resource States do we have?

> **The fact that we have limited memory of childhood indicates that we do not frequent those childhood states**

We have two different types of Resource States. We have surface states and underlying states. Our surface states are those that we switch into and out of through our normal day and week. They are the states we use the most. We have approximately 5 to 15 surface states that we commonly experience life from. While we all have our own distinctive Resource States (one of us might have a comedian state and the other might not), most of us will have some states that carry out tasks that are similar to other people.

Most of us will have a work state that is able to focus on getting work done. We will have a rest state that helps us to not work all the time, and helps us to recharge the body. These two states may not get along if they have not each learned the value of the other.

Other common states many people have are states that like to have fun, states that may do parenting, nurturing or teaching, states that may like an activity such as puzzles or sports, and states that may like sensual pleasures. Our bodies naturally like things like eating and sensuous touch, but we have Resource States that will have developed around those sensual activities.

Some people will have states that do lecturing, states that defend the person by getting angry or upset, and states that may withdraw. We can have a wide array of states and any time you encounter a person, that person is in a Resource State.

We probably have upwards of 100 states in total, as we have many underlying states. Many states that we have developed become underlying states. We have stopped using them often enough so they are no longer surface states.

Some of these we think of as child states. The fact that we have limited memory of childhood indicates that we do not frequent those childhood states. They are still there and they have a lot of memories that we can gain access to. A person may smell something that cues out a childhood state. The person will be able to remember when that was smelled as a child and while that state is out other memories around that time may come back. Hypnotic regression can bring out a childhood state that has very specific memories of childhood.

The subconscious

The subconscious is merely the Resource States that are not currently out, or not currently communicating with the conscious state. States communicate together through synaptic connections; that is, one neural pathway (Resource State) can communicate with another neural pathway (Resource State) when they have a connection.

Our surface states normally have quite good connections between them. If something happens to me when I am in my work state I will tend to remember it when I am in my rest state because those states have a fairly good connection between them. If I learn something in my relaxed study state I will remember most of it when I am tested, in my more nervous state that takes the test, but I may not be able to remember all that my relaxed study Resource State knows. It is a good trick to be able to switch back to the study state to take tests.

Some states do not communicate well together. Sometimes when I am driving I have a state change and I have no memory of driving for the past few minutes. During that time I was obviously in a state that could drive and that state was having its own thoughts, but then I switched into a state that does not have a good synaptic connection with it, then all at once I have no memory of the past few minutes. I had been driving in an underlying state and the surface state I switched into was not able to communicate with the underlying state to get access to the memories of the past few minutes. Those memories are in my subconscious, or in the underlying Resource State that had been driving.

If I can't remember where I put my keys, that information is in my subconscious, and if I can get back into the Resource State that I was in when I put my keys away I can bring that bit of my subconscious, where my keys are, to the conscious.

Multiple Personality

There is a psychological disturbance called dissociative identity disorder (DID) that most people know as multiple personality. A person with multiple personality can have big chunks of the day that they cannot remember. They may meet someone who talks about the good time they had the previous evening, and they may have no memory of ever meeting them. Where a normal person may get up from watching TV, go to the fridge and open the door and then wonder, "What did I come in here for" (lack of communication between states), the DID person may find themselves holding the fridge door open and wonder, "When did I get home, and where have I been for the past few hours."

Multiple personalities are rare. They develop during long-term childhood abuse. Actually, they develop as a coping skill. The child that is abused at night may attempt to not remember that abuse the next day. Over a long period of time this shutting out of what occurred to other Resource States can cause the communication between states, the synaptic connection firings, to atrophy. Lack of use causes the ability for Resource States to communicate together to cease. This is why when a multiple personality person changes states they may not be able to remember what they were doing just a moment before. The ability for communication between many of their states has broken down. Rather than being called Resource States, the states of a person who has multiple personality are called alters, or sometimes personalities.

People with multiple personality can be helped by assisting them to improve communication between their alters. This process takes time, because individuals with multiple personality most often have alters that are distrustful, and that are not aware of each other.

Can we get new Resource States in adulthood?

Most of our Resource States have come from our childhood. They were formed during a time when our brains were growing quickly and when we were discovering new and varied needs. Most of our surface Resource States are actually states that we have had since childhood that we have continued to use. They have collected adult experiences along with childhood experiences, therefore they appear to be adult Resource States. For all practical purposes we can think of them as adult Resource States.

This is not to say that all states come from childhood. New Resource States can be developed if we have a need to repeat something new over and over again, even in adulthood. It is still very common for new Resource States to develop during adolescence. Often, the pressures of adolescence create needs that cannot be satisfied by existing Resource States, therefore new Resource States are formed.

It is more difficult to form new Resource States after childhood, because the brain is not developing as it did. Still, our brains can form new connections right into old age. I will give a couple of examples of Adulthood Resource State formation.

Let's say a man becomes a single father. If this person did not previously develop a nurturing Resource State, it is likely through the repetitive nurturing of his own child that a nurturing Resource State will be developed. Likewise, if a woman who has not previously developed a gutsy, physical Resource State goes into the military then this gutsy, physical Resource State may be developed through the military's basic and continuing training. It is not easy to develop new Resource States in adulthood and it takes considerable effort to do so.

More common than developing new Resource States in adulthood is the retraining of existing Resource States. When we learn a new sport it is most likely that a Resource State that enjoys sports takes on the new sport. If we already have a Resource State with a role similar to a new activity then that existing Resource State will take on the new activity. A Resource State that enjoys preparing food may also take on activities to prepare other things, such as mixing paints when something is going to be painted.

When an activity is not being enjoyed, it is likely that the wrong Resource State is out. For example, if a person has a Resource State that enjoys preparing food, but that person is very tired then a Resource State that has a role of helping the person to rest and recover may be out. This resting Resource State will not be happy about having to prepare food. The person would experience the feeling of an internal struggle. The best way to handle a situation like this would be to have an internal compromise. A set number of minutes for resting might be given to the resting Resource State without interference so the food preparation Resource State can be able to be out later and enjoy fixing of the food.

What happens if a Resource State experiences something scary?

An interesting thing happens when one of our Resource States experiences something scary, or traumatic. Our brains have a need for closure. That is how we learn. We hang onto something until there is a sense that we have learned what we need to know. If we experience something scary or traumatic and we don't get that feeling of closure, a feeling that we understand it and can avoid it in the future, then the Resource State that experienced it will hang onto that negative emotion in and it can bother us again later.

Suppose someone asked me what the name of my first dog was. I may remember the dog really well so if I cannot remember his name I might experience a sense of frustration. I might say to myself, "I know that dog's name. What is it?" I would have the feeling of unease at not being able to remember the dog's name.

Too often things happen, especially with children, that are scary or traumatic, and they are not talked about and understood.

If I did not remember the dog's name, days later something might remind me of that dog again and I would again have that same frustration of not being able to remember the dog's name. That is because that frustrated Resource State comes out and it still does not have closure relating to my first dog's name. As soon as I remember the name, that frustration would disappear completely.

That is an example of how our brains need closure. We need to be able to feel like, "yep, now I've got it," so we can get on with our lives. Not being able to remember a dog's name is not nearly as important or severe as experiencing some sort of traumatic event or a time of feeling really unloved.

If something scary or traumatic happens to us as a child we have a need to talk about it and understand it, and feel supported and nurtured. If this happens then we can pretty much put it behind us. It may remain a bad memory but it is not a continuing piece of unfinished business.

Too often things happen, especially with children, that are scary or traumatic, and they are not talked about and understood. Children may not know they can talk about things, or they may be told not to talk about things, or they may be too scared or embarrassed to talk about things. We all have scary or traumatic things that have happened in our pasts that still affect us today.

I know a woman who almost drowned when she was 10 years old. She was afraid she might be in trouble with her parents if she told them about it, therefore the Resource State that almost drowned and experienced a traumatic incident, did not get any closure, and did not get a sense of support and understanding. She was not able to feel comfortable in the water again, because each time she attempted to go for a swim the traumatized Resource State would come out still feeling the trauma, the unfinished business. She experienced panic attacks when she was in places that reminded her of not getting enough air. She did not know why she had panic attacks, but when her ten-year-old traumatized Resource State was able to gain closure over the incident her panic attacks stopped.

Here is what happens. Let's say I am eight years old and I am in my Resource State that likes to tell jokes and be silly when a tree falls on the house I am in. It is likely that if my joking Resource State would get nurturance and understanding after this , it could feel comfortable and then could continue to joke, possibly even about the tree falling on the house. But if I was in a room I was not supposed to be in when it happened, and if I snuck out and never told anyone I was in the house when the tree came through the wall then that Resource State might not get closure. My joking Resource State would hang onto that fear, having received no nurturance or understanding. This is why crisis intervention is so important after people experience a traumatic incident.

Whenever my joking Resource State came out in the future, which would likely happen at times when the wind blew the trees, or when trees would creak, then I would experience that same sense of fear that was unresolved when the tree hit the house. I would continue to experience this sense of fear during high winds for the rest of my life, unless that 8 year old Resource State was able to get a sense of understanding and nurturance for the frightening incident it had experienced. I might have no knowledge of why the wind frightened me so much.

> **Any time we respond to something in a way that does not fit, there is a reason we responded in the way we did.**

Another consequence of this unfinished business would be, I would no longer be able to enjoy joking because my joking Resource State would be overwhelmed by the frightening incident it experienced.

Remember, if I had been able to get nurturance and a sense of understanding about what had happened, then my joking Resource State would be able to continue with its role of being funny when I needed attention. Because I would not have access to this Resource State to fulfil my attention getting needs, I might have to get attention some other way, like getting into trouble.

When one of our Resource States experiences something traumatic and afterwards gains a sense of nurturance and understanding about it, then that state can continue with its normal function, and we will not continue to be disturbed by the incident. But, when we experience something traumatic and there is no sense of nurturance and understanding afterward, that Resource State hangs onto those negative feelings, just like I hung onto the frustration of not being able to remember my first dog's name. The Resource State has a need for completion and understanding and it hangs onto the negative feelings until it can achieve that sense of completion.

Neuroses

There is a reason for everything. If a person becomes terribly frightened on a windy day, and there is no real danger, and the person knows there is no real danger, but still becomes terribly frightened, then that is a neurotic reaction. We all have neuroses. Any time we respond to something in a way that does not fit, there is a reason we responded in the way we did. The reason is because we have a tender spot on the inside, a Resource State that has unfinished business.

I call a Resource State that has unfinished business a Vaded state. It is a Vaded state because it has been invaded by some kind of fear or trauma. It has not received nurturance and understanding. We all have Vaded states, we all have states that have some level of unfinished business that cause us to respond to some things in a manner that does not really fit the situation.

If a boss at work criticizes our work it could be a normal reaction to feel the criticism is accurate and we need to change something, to feel the criticism is not accurate and we need to explain something to the boss, even to feel the boss is inappropriate in the criticism and is acting in a non-professional way. It is not a normal reaction to feel a sense of hurt and devastation about the criticism that ruins the day. This neurotic reaction comes from a Resource State that was criticized in a frightening manner probably as a child and did not gain a sense of completion afterwards.

I know a man who was unable to speak in front of groups. He would become too nervous to even attempt to speak. When he was a child his father had berated him for not being a good worker, which vaded his 'performance' Resource State. When he thought about speaking in front of a group this performance Resource State would come out with the horrible feelings of 'inability to perform' and 'self-judgment' and he could not speak. After this Resource State was able to gain a sense of nurturance and understanding he was able to speak in front of groups easily. We will learn how to help Vaded Resource States heal later in the book. We have to do more than intellectually understand; the actual Vaded state needs to be able to feel safe and supported.

Can we learn to bring out the Resource State we want out, when we want it out?

The answer is yes. There are times it is easier to learn this than other times.

We often already have some skills in being able to do this. Earlier, I mentioned the weight lifter who can bring out a focused Resource State when lifting weights. The weight lifter does not lift weights when thinking about a math problem, but learns to bring out a state that is quite focused and able to apply energy to lifting the weight. Usually, this bringing out the preferred state is rather easy because no other state is attempting to come out.

If we know we have a state, and we want to bring that state out we can do that easily as long as another state does not want to be out at that time. I gave an example about a man who could not do any public speaking because he had a Vaded state that would jump out with its feelings of being incompetent. Only after that Vaded state became healed could the man bring out his relaxed, communicative state. The Vaded state has a lot of power.

The other instance when it can be difficult to learn to bring out the preferred state is when there is another state that wants to come out to fulfil its function. Let's say you want to get some work done at home after coming home from your job. If you find yourself procrastinating rather than doing the work you want to get done, then there is either a Resource State that wants to use the time for a different purpose, or a Resource State that has some reason for that work not to be done.

You may have a Resource State with a role to help the body rest. This state may be good at being able to tell the body is tired and it may understand how important it is for the body to get some down time so it can regenerate. After a day at work, this state may feel the tiredness of the body and mind and may attempt to come out and help the body to rest. At the same time there is the Resource State that has as its role a need to get some work done, possibly homework, housework, yard work, or something else.

These two Resource States, the 'rest' state and the 'work' state are in inner conflict over what the body will do. When we feel inner conflict like this, it is unsettling. If the rest state is able to come out it is likely that the work state will be in the background berating it with messages about how work needs to be done. This can be experienced as procrastination. In this book we will learn how to help these states learn to respect each other so each can accomplish its purpose without feeling the disdain of the other.

Other things may also interfere with work getting done. There may be a fear of what life will be like if a course of study is finished. If so, the state with this fear might continually find other things to do, rather than work to finish the course. When the course is finished there could be harder work to follow, or there could be a change of relationship with someone important, or there could even be an illogical internal association with finishing a course means being old.

> **It is great to be able to bring a Resource State out that can best enjoy the good things.**

The good news is that we can learn to bring out the desired Resource State when we have peace within. Each of our states needs to learn to be understanding of the others and then in internal compromising can allow our preferred Resource State out. This gives us great power to get things done and to enjoy the good things in life.

It is great to be able to bring a Resource State out that can best enjoy the good things, and to be able to bring a Resource State out that can best accomplish the tasks we want to get done, and it is good to be able to do this without feeling an inner conflict caused by other states wanting to be out at the same time.

Chapter 4: Healthy, Normal Resource States

Imagine feeling inner peace. Imagine being comfortable with who you are, with your potential, and with others around you. Imagine hearing criticism or getting rejection, and being able to reflect on it with wisdom, and without the bad feelings of taking it personally. Imagine being able to go to a park, lay on the grass in the shade, let your head go and really enjoy the feel of the air and the sounds of the birds without any disturbing thoughts or feelings making you feel uncomfortable about being there or worried about what you 'should be doing'. This is what can happen when our Resource States are at peace with each other and are happy. When our Resource States are in a Normal state of being this is what we can have.

Each of our Resource States is in a specific condition of Resource State health. There are four conditions of Resource State health. They are **Normal, Conflicted, Retro, and Vaded**. When a state is in a Normal condition it is healthy and at peace.

The conditions of our states

Normal states

We want our all Resource States to be a Normal condition of health. When our states are in a Normal condition of health they carry out a needed function for us like work, rest, or play, they are respected internally by the other states, and they respect the other states internally.

The working Resource State that provides a service for the person, that is not in conflict with other Resource States internally, and that feels good about itself is in a **Normal** condition.

Conflicted states

Earlier, I gave an example of two Resource States that were **Conflicted**. A work state that wants to do work at home may be conflicted with a rest state that wants to rest at the same time. We can feel this inner conflict. If we are resting we may have the voice of the work state in our head telling us, "You should be doing some work now," and if we are working we may be feeling a need to rest given to us by our rest state. These Resource States are both very useful, and may be good at carrying out their purpose, but they are **Conflicted**.

Conflicted Resource States are quite common. Resource States are Conflicted if the conflict they experience causes us grief and keeps us from being able to get on with life in the way we would like. Conflicted Resource States may keep us up late at night worrying. They disturb our inner peace. They are in an argument with each other. One may say, "I should not be doing what I'm doing," and another may say, "I have to be doing what I'm doing."

Resource States are not Conflicted if they are merely attempting to make a decision. For example, at the supermarket different Resource States may want to buy different things. A number of Resource States may consider what is the best laundry powder to buy, what is the best bread, and how much we want to spend. **Resource States are considered Normal as long as they are carrying out a respectful communication to help us determine what we most prefer**. It is only when their conflict becomes a problem to us that Resource States cease to be **Normal**, and are considered **Conflicted**.

Retro states

Have you ever met someone who becomes angry very easily when criticized or questioned? This person may be very frustrating, because rather than being able to talk openly he or she may quickly go into an angry Resource State. It is likely they are going into a Retro state.

A Retro Resource State is one that has served the person well at some point in life, but because of life changes it no longer continues to serve the person well. If a person is raised in a household where it is necessary to become angry for self-protection, or merely to get what is right, they will likely develop an angry Resource State. This angry Resource State may serve the person well in the household where it was developed. (Note: Anger is a normal human emotion. When I say 'angry state' here I am talking about a state that exhibits an angry attitude in a way that is not helpful to the person. There are appropriate ways to express anger and they will be discussed later in the book.)

The problem begins when this person with an angry Resource State later is living situation where it is inappropriate to display so much anger. Therefore the angry Resource State is carrying out a role that is no longer helpful for the person. Retro refers to something from the past. It is a Retro Resource State that functions as if it were living in the past, and this is not working in the present.

It is possible for Retro Resource States to either learn new skills, or to learn to use their existing skills only during appropriate times. When Retro Resource States are able to do this, when they begin working for the benefit of the person both internally and externally, they become Normal.

Vaded Resource States

I have already spoken some about Vaded Resource States. When a Resource State experiences of fearful or traumatic situation and is not able to gain a feeling of resolution over that then it may become vaded. It is invaded by the fear or rejection, and this becomes its experience each time it comes out.

If a person is in a car wreck and then becomes fearful of driving or riding in a car there is a Resource State that has been vaded. This Resource State comes out when the person either attempts to drive, or to ride in a car. If a child is screamed at for not being able to work properly, and then later in adulthood the person becomes extremely nervous when an employer criticizes their work, there is a Vaded Resource State.

There is great power in resolving Vaded Resource States. There are two very important benefits. When a Resource State that has been vaded can gain resolution then the person is no longer interrupted by the feelings of fear or rejection that sometimes surface, and the Resource State that had been vaded will again be able to carry out its original function. This may mean that the person can become more loving, more playful, or a better student.

The Normal Resource State is not Conflicted, is not Retro, and is not Vaded. The Normal Resource State can only have one condition, being Normal.

> **Whether we are driving, working, having sex, resting, playing, or eating we need to be able to have the state out that gives us the most ability, pleasure, and peace of mind.**

The answer to the question, "What do our states need to be at peace and happy," is really very simple. They merely need to be in the Normal condition. They need our help so that they will no longer be Conflicted, so that they will no longer be Retro, and so that they will no longer be vaded. The good thing is that this can happen.

Conflicted states can learn to respect each other and communicate to compromise, Retro states can learn new roles or to limit their participation to times when it is appropriate that they conduct the role that they know, and Vaded states can receive a sense of nurturance and safety so they can again take on their original roles in a positive fashion.

Three things we need to learn so our states can be Normal

The following unit in this book will cover the three things we need to learn to achieve good mental health. They are each covered in individual chapters.

Chapter 5 is on healing Vaded states. When our upset feelings get in our way, or that we attempt to escape from, we have Vaded states. This chapter is provided to help states move from carrying unresolved upset feelings from the past to being able to feel comfortable and supported. It is about changing Vaded states to Normal states. This may be the most important chapter in this book. It will take a little training to become ready to bring healing to Vaded states but it is well worth it. If you have symptoms of Vaded states, and many of us do, it would be good to read this chapter very carefully, possibly more than once, and spend some time practicing the techniques so you will be ready to use them. The payoff is immense.

Chapter 6 is about making sure we have the right state out at the right time. This is an important chapter for us to learn how to use our internal resources to gain the best experience of life. When we have the wrong state out we may not like what we are doing, and we may do it poorly. We need to match the activity we are doing with the part of us that can do that activity the best, or enjoy it the most. Whether we are driving, working, having sex, resting, playing, or eating we need to be able to have the state out that gives us the most ability, pleasure, and peace of mind.

Chapter 7 is about achieving internal respect among our states. When states are in conflict we can feel like there is a war inside us. It is important for states to learn to respect and honor each other, and for them to continue being different from each other so we have all our internal resources for our benefit. It is also important for Retro states to be able to learn roles the can help us today. That way the states that benefited us in the past can learn to be at peace with other states today and they can learn to be available to us as resources.

Unit 2 is the training unit and it prepares us for what can be changed, in Unit 3. After learning how to change you will be able to find new and creative ways to use these skills that extend beyond the examples.

Unit 2: How to Change

Chapter 5: Healing the Vaded State

There are many advantages to healing our Vaded states. Remember, a Vaded Resource State is one that has been exposed to something frightening or some rejection and then afterward did not gain a sense of closure; support and understanding that allowed that Resource State to 'let it go'.

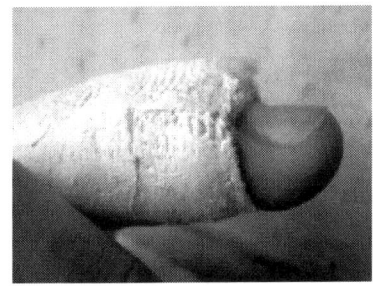

A Vaded state is an unresolved state that is a tender spot in our psyche. When it comes out, gives us a feeling of 'angst' or anxiety that causes us to feel out of control and often causes us to react in a way that we do not feel good about.

A Vaded state, when it comes out with its feeling of anxiety, can cause us to attempt to escape it with drugs, gambling, work, OCD and other zoned out behavior that feels better than the anxiety of the state. Vaded states can bring out feelings of insecurity that cause us to feel a compelling need to compete. Even if we don't want or need something, due to a Vaded state, we may feel we have to

> **Vaded states feel out of control. They feel anxiety.**

have it because of what another person has or because of what we believe they may think. Therefore, healing our Vaded states is very important.

In order to learn how to heal our Vaded Resource States it is important to learn something about what they are like. Here are some traits of Vaded Resource States.

Traits of Vaded States

How they feel:

Vaded states feel out of control. They feel fragile, tender, and sometimes feel angry. When a Vaded state comes out we feel things that do not belong in the present, and they often cause us to interpret things in a strange way. For example, someone may say something slightly critical and we may become very angry or fragile and may have strong feelings, when a slight reaction would better fit what was said.

Where they come from:

Vaded states usually become Vaded in childhood. It is possible that a state may become Vaded in adulthood, with a severe trauma such as a robbery or an accident, but it is more likely that adults have an opportunity to gain an understanding of what they have gone through, especially if some type of caring conversation or trauma counselling took place. When a child experiences something difficult they often do not talk about it. This leaves the Resource State unresolved and hanging onto the feelings of rejection or fear. States may become vaded by a child feeling panic when a parent does not come when called, during an embarrassing moment at school, by feeling lost, or by feeling unloved or rejected. Any event that feels traumatic can vade a Resource State if it is not talked about and understood.

The only way to heal a Vaded state is to work with feelings, not thoughts. Vaded states always have strong feelings and it is through these feelings that they can be healed. It is not possible to help a Vaded state by changing thinking. When we are in an intellectual, thinking Resource State we cannot at the same time be in a Vaded state. If you find yourself considering 'why' then you are not going down a path for healing. The intellectual state may have ideas about why we do things, or about when a Resource State became vaded, but those ideas are often wrong. The only way to heal a Vaded state is to work with that state when it is out and make sure it gains the empowerment, the understanding and the support it needs. Resource State Therapists have techniques to bring a Vaded state out to discover how it became vaded.

We can help heal Vaded states when they come out. This is a very powerful tool to learn. Therapists cannot wait for Vaded states to come out on their own. They would have to follow you around possibly for days waiting for a Vaded state to come out, therefore they have to bring them out in therapy. But, if you are prepared, using the training steps below, you can help heal a Vaded state when it comes out, when you feel the upset feelings it holds.

> **A Vaded state carries with it an illusion.**

For example, if someone says something that makes you feel terrible and you have a disturbing feeling you can't shake, you can use the technique below to help heal the Vaded state that is out at that time. A good thing is that using this technique will help heal the state so it

47

will not bother you as much the next time a similar thing is said to you. Continuing to use the technique can help the state to heal until it becomes 'Normal' and is no longer vaded at all.

What do Vaded States need in order to become Normal States?

A Vaded state carries with it an illusion. It feels the bad thing that happened is still happening, that it is still in danger, or that it is still unloved. In truth, that bad thing is not happening in the present, it is not in the room.

Why continue to empower what has harmed in the past? For example, if a perpetrator has harmed in the past that is bad enough. There is no reason to allow that perpetrator to continue to mess up the life of the victim years later. It is much better to become empowered on the inside, for the state that was vaded to feel safety and support.

We can continue to have the memory of the original event, but we can choose to reclaim the power of our internal world for ourselves. We can change the disempowered 'upset feeling' to a feeling of safety, support and love. There are steps to accomplish this.

3 Steps to heal Vaded states

A Vaded state is not bad or wrong, it is upset. It needs a feeling of acceptance and safety to be Normal. It should not be fought against or pushed away, it should be nurtured. Therefore, the 3 steps to heal a Vaded state are:

1. Find and prepare a nurturing helping state to be ready to help when a Vaded state comes to the surface with its upset feelings.
2. The nurturing state needs to assure the Vaded state that now there is internal safety and that it can clear its inner space of anything that had been upsetting.
3. The nurturing state needs to assure the Vaded state that it is cared about and that it will always be loved on the inside.

If a child is upset it is not helped by being pushed away. The Vaded state is the same. It is helped by feeling safe and supported. To help a Vaded state we need a helping state available when the Vaded state comes out.

Finding a Helping State

We will use the image of helping an upset child to find and bring out a saving, helping Resource State. Read the next paragraphs in a place you can relax and feel comfortable. These are paragraphs that you may want to read many times as you progress through this book. Take time with every sentence to allow each image to become clear. It is important that you experience a helping part of you, wanting to help.

Imagine hearing a child crying. You look around and see a child with eyes filled with tears, sobbing, and just catching breaths between the sobs. A part of you wants to help that child feel better. You look around and see there is no one else there to help. This gives permission to your helping part to approach the child to see what is wrong. The child runs to you and gives you a hug, clinging onto you. This helping part of you gives the child a supportive hug. Love, acceptance, and safety flow from this helping part of you to the child, in an honouring, respectful way. You will make sure that nothing hurts this child.

This loving, supporting Resource State is a great part of you. Let's call it, 'Helper'. Helper is like a big brother, a big sister or a loving parent who will defend the upset child. Helper feels good about helping and about getting appreciation from the upset child. When the child is helped it feels good both to the child and to the helping part.

This part of you, Helper, is key to healing the Vaded state. The upset state is healed by love and support, not by being pushed away. The upset state can gain safety and acceptance from your helping part. It is important for you to get in touch with this Helping part and feel its desire to help the upset child.

Imagine focusing this helping energy into your right hand. Imagine focusing love, acceptance, strength and safety into your right hand, as if it were the hand of god. You are charging your right hand with unconditional acceptance, support and safety, coming from the helping part of you. This right hand state will be able to help move states that have been vaded to feelings of love, support, and safety.

When a Vaded state feels hurt or unlovable you will feel it most in some part of your body.

When help is needed you will just bring the helping hand to the part of the body that feels upset and nurture the part that needs it. When you press this helping hand into the part of you that fills upset your 'Helper' will be sharing a hug. It will be giving love and safety to fill every cell and fibre of the Resource State that feels upset.

When a Vaded state feels hurt or unlovable you will feel it most in some part of your body. For example, it may be felt more in your stomach, chest, neck or head. **Understand that this Vaded state is a child part of you that needs help.** Use the trained, nurturing hand to give it what it needs, even though you may not be feeling like the 'helper' at the time:

When you feel upset do these 3 steps to help resolve a Vaded state:

1. Remember the helping hand is there for you. This is your helping Resource State.
2. Press this hand into the part of the body that feels upset to share unconditional love. The nurturing state needs to assure the Vaded state that the past is powerless and the present is loving. Share loving acceptance as it penetrates unconditionally where it is needed.
3. Allow yourself to feel the connection of the loving helper and the younger Resource State. As the younger Resource State is held with the loving helper it feels the warmth of support and understanding.

This is a very powerful healing process when the helping hand has been charged with a nurturing Resource State and when the love is sent with an intent to heal. This process can be used to help any Vaded state when it is out. Here are some examples:

When a person or incident has made you feel really bad about yourself.

When feeling the uncomfortable compelling feeling to:

- begin OCD behaviour.
- go to a place to gamble.
- take an unwanted drug.
- eat when you are not hungry.
- work beyond a wanted, healthy amount.
- smoke.
- compete.
- buy something you do not really want to buy.
- When you wake up from a disturbed dream.
- When feeling overly nervous before a talk.
- When feeling anxiety about a performance or about competing in sports.
- When feeling anxiety about a dream we just had.

There are many more times when Vaded states come out. A Vaded state is out any time you have a feeling that does not fit the situation you are in, and it is a feeling that is disturbing to you, causing you to feel out of control in some way.

There is no reason for a state to remain vaded when it can become a Normal and healthy state by a process of empowerment, and by becoming clear that it is in a space of safety and support. Resolving Vaded states allows us to become masters of our own lives, no longer ruled by internal fears or feelings of rejection that have in the past compelled us to respond and act in ways that are not really us.

Resolving our Vaded states does not mean we will no longer feel anxiety. Life events are anxiety producing and an appropriate amount of anxiety helps motivate us to respond. There is a difference, though, in anxiety about a present situation that is difficult and anxiety bubbling up from our past that causes us to feel feelings that don't even fit the present situation. If we are not currently threatened by something that could hurt us it is not necessary for us to feel upset.

Forgiveness

How important is it for us to forgive someone who has done us wrong? What a Vaded state needs is a sense of empowerment and support. It needs to gain the realization that its inner space belongs to it and that space is safe and loving. It needs to learn that it can clear out that space and remove absolutely anything that it chooses not to be there. This does not mean that this Resource State needs to forgive.

The Vaded Resource State does not have to forgive a person for anything that he or she may have done, but the Vaded Resource State cannot maintain blame toward the person (a negative, heavy emotion) and at the same time be free. If this Vaded Resource State holds onto feelings of blame that means it is still being impacted negatively because it is not experiencing freedom and lightness.

It is OK to intellectually understand that something is unsafe or that someone should be avoided, but it is not good to continue to be emotionally impacted by the past. An intellectual Resource State can still maintain a non-emotional, intellectual understanding about what has been done. There can be an intellectual blame, just not an emotional blame. The most powerful response to the past is emotional healing.

Think of it this way. If you were in a shop when it was robbed at gunpoint the Resource State that experienced this robbery might become vaded. To heal, this Vaded state needs to be able to totally remove the robber from its inner space and feel support from a nurturing Resource State. If the Vaded state holds the robber inside to constantly say, "I hate you, I hate you," then it is keeping the robber close inside and is not becoming free.

By totally clearing that Resource State's inner space of the robber it can become free of those negative feelings. There has been no forgiveness, but the state that had been vaded also has no emotional feelings of blame toward the robber, because it has no feelings at all toward the robber. The robber has been emotionally removed. Any power the robber had on the inside to upset has been removed. Another intellectual Resource State can still understand the crime and even pursue charges, but the personality is free of the trauma and can move forward.

Let's look at another example. Let's say that Frank's father

> **The Vaded state carries the baggage of negative feelings.**

screamed at him and told him that he was worthless, a complete failure, and that he would never amount to anything. The Resource State that Frank was in at the time did not talk to anyone about it. This Resource State with its very low self-concept would later come out when an authority figure was critical of Frank. Frank would have the same feelings that he did when his father screamed at him. He would feel incompetent and feel like he would never amount to anything. He would feel these things because this Vaded Resource State that was unresolved would come to the surface with its unresolved feelings. This Resource State needed a sense of resolution, support, and love.

When it is out, Frank's Vaded Resource State can get nurturance (unconditional love) it can learn that the experience of being yelled at by his father is in the past and gone, and it can gain a feeling of support and love from the nurturing Resource State that is there to help him through the helping hand.

This process involves Frank's becoming empowered and clearing his inner space making it nice and safe and secure. It does not involve forgiveness.

There is a similarity between forgiveness and letting go of the negative feelings. Frank is letting go of the negative feelings by clearing his inner space and leaving only positive things in that space. This Resource State that had been vaded is left with an experience of support and love from the helping state, and it is not hanging onto any fear or blame. It is happy. The happy Resource State is not hanging onto negativity or blame. It is experiencing love and support from the helping Resource State.

Frank may have other Resource States that understand what his father did was inappropriate and wrong. As long as they are not vaded that is not a problem. Our intellectual Resource States that can understand, without emotion, are very useful.

Sometimes clients ask me if they should bring charges against someone who has wronged them. I tell them that that is up to them, that if they want to I will support them, but that has nothing to do with the therapy. Becoming free is letting go, not maintaining attachments. It is imperative that Vaded Resource States let go. It is OK for other Resource States to maintain a communication or to make criminal charges. And, obviously, if someone else is in current danger it is important that steps be made to help protect any innocent person.

The Vaded state has carried an image of person or a thing that caused the negative feelings. Becoming internally empowered and accepted and getting the sense of freedom from anything negative is what moves the previously Vaded state to being a Resource State in a Normal condition. This happens all internally and how any current relationship is handled externally is up to the more mature and assertive Resource States.

Chapter 6: Making sure we have the right Resource State out

We have just learned how to help Vaded states. That is something we have to be able to do before we can make sure we have the best state out for our purpose. A state that is vaded can force itself out making us feel out of control, so we need to make sure that our Vaded states are healed, or at least getting what they need before we can make sure that we have the best state out.

It is not really difficult to bring out the state that we want. We just need to learn our inner resources and get inner permission for them to come out when we need them.

We will use an example to help you see how you can make sure you get the best state out. Let's say you hate washing dishes. When you wash dishes you are resentful and you think about other things you would rather be doing. Your time seems wasted and you can't wait to finish. If this is the case, you have the wrong Resource State out while you're washing dishes. You may never truly wish you had more dishes to wash, but there is no reason why washing dishes can't be an acceptable experience when you do them.

Determining which state is out

> **It is not really difficult to bring out the state that we want.**

First, sit down and make yourself comfortable. When you become comfortable and relaxed think about standing in front of the sink washing dishes. This thought will probably disturb your relaxation somewhat. That is good. Allow yourself to feel the frustration of washing dishes, in the same way you would normally feel it.

While in this state, ask yourself, "What can I call this part of me? What name or term would fit this part?" Let's say the name that comes to you is, 'Frustrated'. You can now say directly to this part, "Frustrated' you will never have to wash another dish for as long as you live." This is true because this state is not the best state for you to be washing dishes with. You will be much better having another state out when you wash dishes.

Determining the qualities of the state you want out

Now, think of the process of washing dishes. Think of what happens with that activity. It is fairly mindless, you have your hands in warm water, you are able to see dirty dishes become clean, and you are able to move things around and stack them. What kind of part might either enjoy or be more okay with this type of activity.

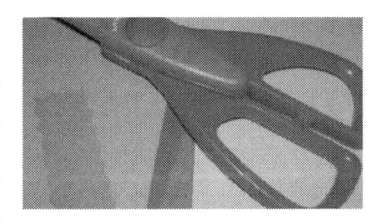

Working in warm water, making dirty things clean, and stacking things sounds like an activity that a craft-like state would enjoy. You may have a state that hasn't been given much time to work with crafts, to be a bit mindless, and to enjoy the feel of warm water on the hands. This is the type of state that you are looking for.

Finding the right state

Think of a time in your life when you have enjoyed this type of 'craft-like' activity before. It may have been in childhood, or it may have been last week. Let's say, as a child, there was a time when you would find things in the sand on the beach and you would enjoy taking them back and washing them off and seeing how new looking you could make them.

Bringing the Resource State out

Okay, you have found a state that you can use. Now you need to bring that state out so you can get an agreement from that state that it will help you when you want to wash dishes. In order to bring this state out you really need to get as much focus on what it felt like to wash off those things you found on the beach as you can. Think about the feel of the water, and the excitement of discovering what these beach objects will be able to look like when they are clean. Think about the timeless nature of just being there with the objects you were washing, how in a way it is both exciting and relaxing. Think about what you could call this part of you that has this feeling of being there enjoying the water and the craft-like behavior.

While feeling what it feels like to be in this Resource State, think about a good name for this part of yourself. Let's say the name that comes to you is, 'Crafty'. It may be nice being in this crafty state of yours and feeling what it feels like to be crafty. Now that you are in your crafty state ask this part of you if it would be willing to come out and help you feel more positive while you are washing dishes. This doesn't mean you should wash any more dishes than you already do, but it means that if you are going to be washing dishes you might as well be in this crafty state that can better enjoy the time, the feel of the water, and the experience of timelessness.

Listen to see what this crafty part of you says when you ask it if it will be willing to help you with the dishes. Parts really do enjoy having time where they are out and doing things. It is most likely that this part will be very happy to have more time out.

Checking for objections

We are almost done. The last thing that needs to be done is to make sure that no other Resource States will object to Crafty being out when the dishes are being washed. For example, if a partner has told you to wash the dishes you may feel some resentment and there may be a part of you that does not want to feel okay about washing dishes. This part might object to Crafty coming out and feeling okay about the experience.

Here is how to check to see if there are any objections from other Resource States. Sit quietly and close your eyes and imagine a time when you would likely be washing dishes. Using your imagery, invite Crafty to come out to wash the dishes. As you begin to experience Crafty washing the dishes test how you are feeling. Does Crafty have permission from all your other Resource States to be out? Is there an inner peace about Crafty being the one that is now washing the dishes? If there is, then you can just enjoy having a better state at your disposal to do the task of dishwashing. The state that you earlier named Frustrated will likely very much enjoy being able to do what it wants, and never again wash dishes.

If there is a state that has a problem with Crafty washing dishes, that state needs to be negotiated with. For example, if there is a state that feels resentful about washing dishes you might tell it that you will make sure that you will not be washing any more dishes than you otherwise would, and there is no reason you shouldn't be enjoying the time while you wash the dishes.

To be resentful toward someone else would just be allowing them to make your world more upset. That would empower them, and that is not what you would like to do. If you choose not to wash the dishes, then you can say no, but if you decide that you are going to wash the dishes you might as well be as comfortable and happy during that process is possible. Why not have a comfortable and happy life, whenever possible?

What if you cannot find a state that has the qualities that you need?
Sometimes we want a state to help us with something and we cannot find a state that has those abilities. For example, what would have happened if when we looked for a crafty state we could not find one that we had ever experienced in our life?

This is not a problem. If we cannot find a state that appears to have the qualities that we need for a particular task or to relate to someone at a particular time all we need to do is think of how our ideal person would handle that situation. What would be the perfect way of handling the situation? This is the question to ask ourselves. Then listen for the answer.

One way of doing it is to start writing down how the ideal person would deal with the situation that we have. Another way is just to start thinking about how the ideal person would deal with this kind of situation. While you are answering this question you have a Resource State out that really has a good handle on how the particular situation should be managed. This is the exact state that can help you manage the situation, even if it has never had that role before. It is the best state because it really understands how the situation you are thinking about should be handled.

So, after writing or listening to your state define exactly how the situation should be handled, stop and asked this part what would be a good name for it. What term or name really fits this part of you?

Then, call this part by name and ask it, "Even though you may not have done this type of thing before would you be willing to help me when this situation arises? You would be very useful to me." Here, one of your Resource States is asking for help from another state.

As I mentioned above, states love to come out and have an activity. It is highly likely that this state that you now know the name of, and that you have addressed by its name, will be happy to come out and help you in the future when it is needed.

Here are the Steps explained above to make sure you have the right state out. They correspond with the sections above.

1. Find the state that is coming out now, the state that is not the best state to have out for the activity you are doing.
2. Determine the qualities of the state you want out.
3. Find the best state to have out for the activity you are doing, get a name for it and get it to agree to help you with your current need.
4. Check to make sure that no other Resource States (including the state in Step 1) have a problem with the preferred state coming out, and get an internal handshake with all states involved.

These techniques should work well. If they do not, or do not continue to work it is likely that a Vaded state is involved with unprocessed feelings that block the preferred state from coming out. If this is the case attend to this feeling, Vaded state with the techniques in Chapter 5 above on 'Healing the Vaded State'.

Chapter 7: Achieving respect among our states, Peace Within

We have all experienced hearing an argument in our head. These arguments can make us feel very uncomfortable. They can make us feel we should be working rather than what we are doing. They can make us feel unsettled, and they definitely keep us from having an inner peace.

Moving our inner argument to a discussion

It is important to know the difference between an argument and a discussion. We want our Resource States to be able to discuss things together. If we are going to get married we want to be able to hear from Resource States that know about love, sex, finances, expectations, and common sense. We want to hear from all Resource States with these abilities so we can feel comfortable with our big decision.

What we don't want is an argument where parts of us do not respect other parts of us. "I hate myself when I'm like that," is an

> **It is important to know the difference between an argument and a discussion.**

example of the statement where one Resource State does not respect another.

As mentioned earlier in this book, many of us have a Resource State that needs to recharge the body by resting and another Resource State that wants to get work done and often these two Resource States do not really know or understand each other. The work state may think of the resting state as lazy, and the resting state may think of the work state as a mindless slave driver.

This is not good for our inner peace. It is not good for our ability to rest, and it is not good for our ability to get work done.

It would be much better if these two states respected each other so that the resting state could have some time to rest deeply without hearing complaints in the head, and the work state has some time to get work done while the body is filled with energy.

It is good to be able to feel at peace inside. This is a feeling that comes when Resource States know each other, respect each other, and learn to compromise and work together. When one Resource State does an action that other Resource States do not appreciate we are not able to sit down and feel really positive about ourselves. Low internal respect and poor Resource State communication lead to this. Here is an example.

Let's say Mia finds Ben attractive. Ben is married and Mia wants to respect that. She honors the institution of marriage and doesn't see herself as someone who would do anything to compromise it. One night at a party Mia and Ben are out on the deck talking. They began kissing, which feels really right at the time and good to Mia. But, just a few minutes later Mia's other

Resource States come out and berate her for what she has done. She feels awful. She has no peace within.

Here is what happened. Mia had a Resource State that found Ben very attractive and wanted to be with him. This Resource State did not communicate well with Mia's other Resource States, and did not take their opinions into consideration. When it got a chance to kiss Ben it took that chance and it used it to its advantage. It did not care about Mia's other Resource States. Afterward the other Resource States had no respect for what Mia's 'needing love' Resource State had done. They chastised that state and said it was bad.

Mia may even have states that say different things to different people. For example, when talking to Ben Mia may tell him about the positive feeling she feels for him, but while talking to another friend she may tell a very different story. She may even tell two different friends that they each are the most important person to her, and each time she says this it may feel like it is the total truth to her.

> **Our states have their own specific abilities and interest, and that brings the richness to our lives.**

It is the total truth to the Resource State that is saying it. But when Mia is not consistent in what she says to people this causes her to lose respect for herself and causes other people to lose respect for her also.

It is deeply satisfying to feel like an honorable person. When each Resource State honors the others on the inside then there can be a consistency on the outside. It is good when our group of states can speak externally with a single voice. They can achieve that voice through compromise and internal respect.

As we learned in the last chapter, we want to have the right Resource State out at the right time. This gives us the greatest opportunity to both enjoy and do well in life. It is also good when no matter which Resource State is out, what it says and does is respected by the other Resource States. Then we can have peace within.

Helping Resource States to know and respect each other

So how do we do this? How do we get our different states to know and respect each other? We definitely do not want our states to all be the same. Our states have their own specific abilities and interest, and that brings the richness to our lives. We want our different states and we want them to be different from one another, we just want them to respect each other and all get along.

We want them to learn to compromise. We want each of our states to think about the other states when making decisions, and make decisions accordingly. We want each state to feel good about itself, to see that it has an important role, and to know that the other states have important roles too.

The first step in having inner peace is to know that these are the things we want, different states with different roles that get along, having respect for each other and compromising with each other. Once we have this vision and know that this is what we want then we are ready to begin the process of change.

You will need two chairs. Think about two parts of yourself that have inner conflict; two voices that don't agree. They are both important.

The steps to inner respect
1. Set down in one of the two chairs and ask yourself which of these two parts of yourself feels most here right now in this chair? This is the first Resource State you will work with, so concentrate only on the thoughts and feelings of this one state.
2. While thinking about how you feel about being in this Resource State, ask this Resource State what would be a good name for itself. It is best if the Resource State chooses its own name so it will feel comfortable with that name.
3. Internally, ask this Resource State what it does for you, how it helps you, what its role is. You need to appreciate that this Resource State is there to help you.
4. Ask this Resource State, calling it by the name that it has given you for itself, what it thinks about the other Resource State that will be speaking from the other chair.
5. Thank it for its opinion, then stand up, and move to the other chair. When you sit down in the other chair you

are in the place for the other Resource State to speak. Concentrate only on the thoughts and feelings of this other state.

Do steps 2, 3, and 4 above with this Resource State.

Call this Resource State by its name is given and let it know how important it is and also how important the other Resource State is. Let it know how the two of them will be stronger by respecting each other and working together.

Considering these things, ask it what it would like to say directly to the other Resource State.

Have it speak directly to the other chair, to the other Resource State. As this happens you should be speaking out loud directly to the other chair. What you are after is appreciation and compromise, and for each Resource State to get an understanding of the importance of the other.

Continue the conversation, moving back and forth between the chairs, helping each state to understand the other and compromise with the other, ending with an internal handshake and commitment that the two states will work together in the future internally.

During the above process it is most important that the two states speak out loud and directly with each other. Often a compromise is achieved with each Resource State getting some time to do what it does without the interference of the other, and for each Resource State to acknowledge the value of the other. It is important that the Resource States feel they can continue to communicate together on the inside. That way your actions will reflect the compromise of all your states, actions that you will feel good about later.

Usually, Resource States help make it possible for each other to do what they need to do, but often they do not understand that. For example, a work Resource State, by working, makes it possible for the person to have time to rest, and a resting Resource State, by resting, recharges the body and keeps it healthy making it possible for the work Resource State to work.

You can do this process any time you feel hostility between two parts of yourself. Of course, you will have to have some time and space to be able to do this.

By continuing to work with Conflicted Resource States in this way you will get to the point where you no longer have Resource States that disrespect each other. Some states may want different things, but the needs of each are important and they need to find a way to compromise. When each of your states respect all other states then you have inner peace, and then it will be easy to present yourself to the world as a together person.

Vaded states

When you are working to help all of your states respect and get along with each other you may find states that feel a negative emotion and that are unable to compromise. These are Vaded states. They can be helped using the steps in Chapter 5 on healing Vaded states. After the Vaded states have become Normal states then they will be able to compromise and respect other Resource States.

Retro States

Retro states are those Resource States that are continuing to operate as they did in the past, even though it no longer works for you today. These states will almost always be conflicted with other states. They need to learn to change their roles so that they can get along with other states, and so they will help you today in getting along with other people.

A Retro state had an original role that no longer works for the person. They do not feel out of control, as Vaded states do, they just feel like their role is important and that it is what they know to do. At first Retro states may believe they cannot change their role, but they can. For example, a Retro state that has in the past shown out of control anger can change its role from coming out quite often to coming out only when the body is in physical danger. If the body is about to be attacked by wild dogs, or down an alleyway by a group of thugs then it would be useful and appropriate for this state that can show out of control anger to come out and help save the body. But, if we are just communicating with people who we know it is not useful for this state to come out and embarrass us and get us in trouble with our friends or acquaintances. It is not good for our friends either!

Therefore, it is good to negotiate with Retro states so they can take a smaller role and come out only when it is appropriate, or to tweak their roles so that they will be appreciated. It will feel good to them to be appreciated on the inside and it will allow you to feel more inner peace. When I say 'negotiate' with them what I mean is for you to have two chairs and have a Resource State that wants to help the Retro state change speak from one chair, and use the other chair to allow the Retro state to speak. Always show respect to all states.

Normal states

Remember, the goal is to help all states to be Normal, that is not Conflicted, non-Vaded, not Retro. The goal is not to have all states think and feel the same thing, but to have all states respect and honor each other so that internal compromises can be made that will be best for us.

If a Resource State really wants a piece of chocolate and can communicate with the state that is watching the diet a compromise may be made. You may be able to have a piece of chocolate that is big enough to gain pleasure, but not too big to blow the diet.

We need and should want all of our states doing their roles. They protect us, help us enjoy living, hold the intellect that we use, and provide us with well-rounded lives. Having different states is very useful.

Respect Within

Everything does not happen immediately. We may not see today what we need to change tomorrow. It is good to give ourselves a break and also, as much as possible, give others a break. When we feel a hardness in us, or see it in others, it is good to know that beneath that, are Resource States that are fragile and gentle.

The Roughened Shell

In life, I touched a shell so large,

With points so rough, and skin so hard,
My touch was pain and plain disgust,
That such a thing was here to touch.

Yet, there it stood, in front of me,
Rough, ugly, sharp and grey.
How dare that cutting, hurting thing,
Come back and be that way?

My hate was peaked.
My fear was marked.
My action unwithstrained.
And what my action was,
Was more than I had dreamed.

Strike once, and twice,
My words came down,
With might upon the shell.

But, what I saw beneath the rough,
I shudder, yet, to tell.

Inside that thing, I hated such,
That destruction filled my mind,

Lay smooth and fragile tinted parts,
Of an awe, and wonder kind.

And when I see the roughened shell,
Upon the beach of life,
I think of how beneath the rough,
There lies a beauty shrine.

Unit 3: What can be changed?

Chapter 8: Weight

Talk about internal fights. Many of us have internal fights among our Resource States when it comes to eating and being able to weigh what we want. Probably the most common food issue people have is eating more than they want to. Stepping on the scales or looking in the mirror brings out one Resource State that wants a different body, then there is that other Resource State that may be out when food is tempting.

Let me paint the picture with a bit more detail. Some of you may be able to identify, and even if you don't experience eating as an issue you may have a problem that is similar, one where you tend to do things at one time and feel bad about it at other times. Here is a common scenario.

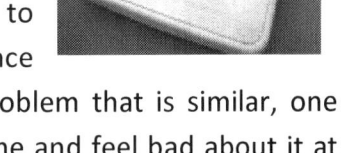

Emma looks down at her body and sees fat that she detests. She may feel so bad about her weight that she will step onto the scales only in private, or she may not even weigh herself at all. She is afraid of what she might see on the scales. She does not want to face it and does not want to have confirmed what she already knows. In the bathroom she sees herself in the mirror and hates what she sees. She has clothes that do not fit her and she does not want to buy new clothes to fit her current size.

She says to herself, "That's it. From now on I am only going to eat low fat foods and I am going to exercise every day. I'm going to stay away from sweet things and eat more vegetables. I am going to become what I want to be. I am going to become the weight I want to be." If we were to name this state that is talking in Emma's head 'Health' might be a good name for it.

> **From now on I am only going to eat low fat foods and I am going to exercise every day**

The next day Emma comes home from work, tired, wrung out, and somewhat hungry. She feels empty in more ways than just being hungry. Her body leads her to the fridge, and her Health state closes down feeling a bit in a fog with Emma just hearing an internal voice saying, "It's OK to have this food now. I will start with the healthy stuff a bit later, or I will go for a long walk later. I really need this food now. If I don't have it I might get sick."

She eats a little and keeps eating and keeps returning for more food. Her body feels like it is telling her she needs it, and that it is OK. The part of her that had stood on the scales and looked in the mirror, 'Health', is roped, tied, gagged and hidden in the corner of her psyche. An eating Resource State is now in control.

Obviously, Emma has Conflicted Resource States. One state wants a healthy diet, and one state wants to give the body food.

In truth, the body may not want it. It has been trained to expect it. I will give you an example.

Be careful about giving your body what it asks for

I am addicted to coffee. I know this and I accept it because coffee can improve certain aspects of health, although it is unhealthy in some other ways. Maybe in the future I will learn something that will convince me to end my addiction, but for now I am physically addicted and feel OK about the amount of coffee I drink.

If I do not have a coffee by two o'clock in the afternoon I get a bad headache and get flu like symptoms, feeling drained and ill. If I do not drink coffee for two or three days my legs ache so much it is difficult to sleep. It would be easy for me to say that my body wants coffee. In truth, my body is mindless.

I have a physical body that has been trained by me to expect coffee. It expects it so much that if I do not drink a cup it makes me feel physically bad. If I were to decide not to have a cup of coffee for one day my body would start feeling withdrawal symptoms. That is my physical body feeling those symptoms, not a Resource State. It is true that a Resource State is out when my body feels the symptoms, but it is the body that feels them, just like it would feel the pain if I stubbed my toe.

I have a Resource State that is responsive to my body, one that likes to give in to my body. When my body is well trained, that works pretty nicely. My body says it is thirsty so my responder Resource State gives it something to drink. My body says it is tired and my responder Resource State attempts to give my body rest. It works pretty well, unless my body has been trained to expect something that is not good for it, and not what I really want to have. This is what happens to me with coffee. I have trained my body to expect something that may not be good for it. This is what happens with people who have bad eating habits. The body learns to expect the food that may not be good for it.

I was raised drinking full cream milk. The first time I tasted skimmed milk, it tasted terrible to me. My body was trained to expect the fat in milk. Now I only drink skimmed milk and if I taste full cream milk it tastes terrible to me. I really don't like it. But if I were to force myself to drink it for a period of time then my body would begin expecting it.

For years I had two spoons of sugar in my coffee and when I tasted coffee without sugar it tasted awful. Now I don't add sugar to anything. When I taste coffee with sugar in it I really hate the taste. I love the taste of coffee without sugar, and it seems like it has a lot more taste now that it is not hidden behind the sugar.

I think you may get the point. Our bodies grow to expect certain things and when they don't get what they have learned to expect they demand it from us. This can be a bit confusing as some people say they listen to their bodies to know what is right to eat. I think it is true that our bodies will crave certain foods that are healthy, but our bodies will also crave foods that are not good for us, just because we are used to them.

Our bodies can be trained by spending a period of time eating what is healthy. It would be nice if that were the only issue with eating more than we really want to eat. If it were, all we would have to do is force ourselves to eat better food for a month and the rest would be easy. For some people it can be that simple, but for others there are other things involved.

The Set Point Theory

There is the issue that some people call the set point. This is the theory that at birth our bodies are pre-programmed to be a certain size, which includes height and weight. There is some evidence to support this and some evidence that indicates that even if this is so, we still have an ability to be closer to the weight we choose than to our set point weight.

Occasionally we see a group of siblings who were adopted out, each at birth and then reunited in adulthood, after living lives completely independent of each other. Often they did not even know they had siblings until one of them did research and found out. When these siblings re-unite it is most often amazing how their body types and weights are similar.

It appears they are just as similar as siblings who have been raised together. This would indicate that there is something to the set point theory. If siblings raised separately in different families wind up with similar body types and weights then genealogy must be a powerful force in determining weight.

> **Since social pressure can have an impact on our weight, our set point can be changed.**

Indeed it is, but we do sometimes see siblings who are

significantly heavier or lighter than their other siblings. This could be due to normal genetic differences, just as differences in hair color. It could also be due to something about where or how they were raised, or even to their own decisions.

There are often parts of a country where the average weight is quite a lot more or less than other parts of the same country. My weight is in the healthy range according to medical height-weight charts, but when I go back to where I was raised I am constantly told that I need to fatten up, that I am just skin and bones, or that I need to put some meat on my bones.

Large portions of food are placed in front of me, and there is a real pressure to eat more. This is the case, even though I am not skinny and I fall right in the middle of the doctor's height-weight charts indicating that I do not need to gain weight.

Most of my friends and relatives who live there have a weight that is normal for that area, but a weight that would be considered as unhealthy by nutritionists. This indicates that social pressure can have an impact on our weight, and that it is not all a result of a set point.

Another cultural factor that seems to influence weight is which foods are eaten. We are told to eat less fat and more vegetables. Many Asian cultures predominantly serve food that has more vegetables and less fat. There seems to be fewer overweight people when people follow those diets. Countries that have diets high in fat tend to have more people who are fat. This is not rocket science, but it does point to the fact that both social pressure and social eating habits impact on our weight. It indicates that everything is not dependent on the set point.

If there were nothing we could do to vary our weights from the set point we had at birth then we would be powerless. But, if where we live influences our weight and if the cultural type of food we eat influences our weight then obviously our weight can be changed from its set point.

We can change our weight, and we can change it without having to move or without hiring an Asian cook. Working with our Resource States gives us the power to change ourselves, physically.

Three reasons we are overweight

We cannot change our set point, but we have seen that the types of foods eaten and social pressure also causes our weights to vary. It is useful to focus on what we can change. That is what the following paragraphs do.

There are really three reasons we sometimes weigh more than we would like.

>**Habit:** We may have a habit of eating the wrong things so we crave the wrong things. Our bodies demand what they are used to.
>
>**Social Pressure:** Social pressure is another reason some people eat more than they would like. This includes family and friends who pressure us to eat either more food than is healthy or a type of food that is not healthy, "You have to have this (large piece of my Chocolate Mud Cake)." The culture in which we live can also pressure us to eat foods that are not the best type, and it can also pressure us to eat too much.

Resource States need Healing: We may also eat more than we want because of Resource States that have unresolved issues. It is good to discover this, because we can do something about it to get the change we want. A Vaded Resource State can cause us to eat to escape the bad feelings we would be feeling if we were not covering them up by eating. We may eat to escape the bad feelings of a Resource State, or we may eat to protect a frightened Resource State. One way to feel safer from being approached by an admirer is to cover the body with an insulating layer of fat.

The section below on eating to escape explains more about how Resource States can impact our eating.

Eating to escape

There are two kinds of addictions. There are physical addictions, where the body is trained to expect something and it makes us feel bad if it

> **There are two kinds of addictions, physical and psychological.**

does not get what it expects. My coffee addiction is an example of this. Anyone can have a physical addiction, and we probably all do. There are also psychological addictions. This is when we have an addictive personality. An addictive personality does not need to be permanent, but it will be unless it is addressed. Many people overeat because they have an addictive personality.

An addictive personality is caused by a Resource State that feels really bad, it feels anxious. When this Resource State comes to the surface we feel anxiety, bad feelings, and we don't want to. We want to escape that bad feeling, and often we escape it in a way that allows us to zone out into a safe place. As discussed above, a Resource State that has taken on bad feelings and has not resolved those feelings is called a Vaded state.

Let's say Emma has a Vaded state. Let's say when she was a little girl she was in a room where she felt alone and frightened and she called out for one of her parents and they never came. She continued to call and no one came. This state that was calling became extremely frightened and panicked. Afterward, after experiencing this panic, it did not get a feeling of resolution so it held onto this deep lonely, helpless, panic feeling.

Now, as an adult sometimes when Emma comes home from work, the house is empty and this unresolved, needy, panic feeling Resource State comes to the surface. This is a feeling Emma does not want. Subconsciously, she has discovered that if she can zone out by eating she can escape the bad feelings of this panic feeling Vaded Resource State. Therefore she when she enters her empty house she feels compelled to go to the fridge and get something to eat. She may feel compelled to keep eating until she had eaten much more than her 'Health' state would want.

If Emma is eating because of a Vaded Resource State she will not be able to merely change her habit, because if she tried to just stop eating the amount and kinds of foods she is used to eating, she would be removing her coping mechanism of going into a safe place of 'eating and eating'. Her Vaded Resource State would begin to flood her with those bad panicky feelings and she would do just about anything to get relief. Eating would seem like a small price to pay for escaping from the feelings of the Vaded state.

This is not something Emma thinks about, it is something she has discovered subconsciously. When Emma eats she can taste something (food) and do something (eat) and this helps her to zone out away from the Vaded state. The only way for her to really break her overeating is to heal the Vaded state so she no longer has to escape from it, then learn new habits. We will learn how to do this.

Eating to hide

A Vaded state can cause Emma to overeat in another way too. Let's say something has happened in Emma's life that causes her to fear being approached by men or women who find her attractive. It could be something that has given her a fear of abuse, or it could be something that has given her a fear that she might do something she would not feel good about. She might fear her ability to control herself if she was approached as an attractive person. She may feel out of control when approached as a sexy person.

If she does feel out of control in this way a good way for her to feel safe is to avoid being approached. It could be frightening to her to be attractive. One Resource State might really want to be sexy, but another Resource State might fear being approached. If this is the case this frightened Resource State will want to make sure Emma eats enough to protect herself from being approached.

If this is why Emma overeats she must learn to become comfortable with being attractive. She must learn to feel in control of situations where she is found attractive by a person who might proposition her in some way.

What might cause a person to fear being attractive? Many things can cause this, but a Vaded state is normally involved. Let's say as a little girl Emma had a sister who became angry at her for 'getting too much', or in her sister's words, for 'being the favourite'. Emma's sister may have been very upset with her and may withdraw her love from her, causing Emma to feel a real loss, because she was 'too good'.

This sad, unloved Resource State of Emma's may attempt to fail so it can be accepted. It carries the message 'fail to get love', and 'succeed and lose love'. This 'fail to get love' Vaded Resource State can insure that Emma does not look too good, in fear of losing love. It does not matter if it has nothing to do with the present, the Resource State can still carry those feelings from the past.

Another example of a state that may fear being attractive is a state that has been frightened by the attention of others. This could be associated with abuse, and it can also just be associated with getting attention and not knowing how to deal with it.

For example, Emma may have been flirted with at a time when she did not know what to do. She may have felt extremely uncomfortable and afraid of doing the wrong thing. She may have feared doing something that would be against her beliefs, or she may have even feared doing something that would upset 'God'. This immense discomfort with attention may have vaded a Resource State. That Vaded state may want Emma large enough so she will not have to be tempted. If Emma starts looking sexy this state can compel her to eat until she feels safe again.

Even being abused can vade a state in such a way that it feels safer with a protective layer of fat that could discourage a potential abuser.

It is becoming clear that there are often different reasons we may eat more than we want, more than is healthy.

> **A vaded state screams out for healing and it will not rest until it gets it, no matter how much we want to change a habit.**

Changing the amount we eat

It is good to know why we eat what we do, but how do we change it? The changes have to be made in the right order otherwise they will not work, and that can make us feel powerless.

The very first step is to find if a Vaded state is involved in our eating and resolve that issue before moving to any other issue. If a Vaded state is causing us to eat more than we want we cannot just change our habit. If we try to change our habit the Vaded state will still have a need for us to eat and therefore we will.

Vaded states can easily overpower our will. A vaded state is screaming out for healing and it will not rest until it gets it, no matter how much we want to change a habit.

Therefore, it is almost impossible to overpower a Vaded state, and if we do it takes much, much effort. And we would have to continue with that effort day in and day out. We should not try to overpower a Vaded state. We should heal the state so it is no longer Vaded, then we will be free to break the unwanted habit that has been fed by the state that had previously been vaded.

The steps to learn to eat what we want

The three steps to eat what we want and no more than what we want are:

1. Check and see if a Vaded state is involved in our eating, and if it is resolve it,
2. Learn how to respond to pressure, and
3. Learn how to break habits of eating the wrong types of food.

Step 1: Determine if our eating is caused by a Vaded state

Another way of saying this is, we need to determine if something from our past is causing us to feel upset in such a way that we eat what we don't really want to eat in order to cover up the bad feelings. If it is, then we need to complete this first step and bring peace to the Vaded state before going to step 2. If we find that a Vaded state is not affecting our eating then we can go straight to step 2.

How to determine if our eating is affected by a Vaded state

If, while you are eating what you do not want to eat, you are feeling zoned out and out of control, then a Vaded state is probably involved. If, while you are eating what you do not want to eat, you are feeling hungry and in need of the food you are eating to stop your body from craving, then a Vaded state is probably not involved.

We all at times feel hungry. The big factor that will tell us if a Vaded state is involved is if there is a significant amount of time when we feel we are escaping with food, if we are eating in a spaced out zone that gives us a level of safety, then we need to heal a Vaded state. If this is the case, look at Chapter 5 in unit 2 of this book on '**Healing the Vaded State**'. Use the techniques in that chapter each time you feel compelled to eat something you do not want. After the Vaded state is healed you will no longer feel this compulsion.

Also, we can feel compelled to please other people because we have a Vaded state.

How to determine if our feeling pressured is caused by a Vaded state

If, when you give in to pressure to eat you feel out of control, if you feel a level of powerlessness, and if you feel a bit like a child needing to please, then you are responding from a Vaded state. If, when you give in to pressure you feel a warmth toward the other person and you do not feel 'a need to please', if instead you feel a positive feeling then you are not responding from a Vaded state. If you do feel compelled to please, use your nurturing hand from Chapter 5 to quell those feelings when they come out.

Step 2 is about responding to pressure to eat just because we want to please, even though we do not feel compelled to please. It is helpful to respond to the pressures of others by making sure we have the right assertive Resource State out when we are being pressured.

Step 2: How to bring the right state out to respond to pressure

We all have Resource States that want to please. There is nothing wrong with that. At the right time it feels good to be helpful or nurturing, and it is good for our careers to please 'the boss'.

There are times when it is appropriate to please and times when we would later feel bad about compromising ourselves in some way. Probably the best test of, 'When is it right to please?' is thinking about how we will feel about it later. If later we will regret our giving in to another person then it is not the right time to please. If later we will feel good about our actions then it probably was a good time to be giving or nurturing.

There may even be times when it is appropriate to please others in what we eat. It is often nice to taste what someone has prepared, bought, or brought. Often it does not corrupt our diet to do so.

There are times, though, that we give in to others and eat what we really do not want, then later wish we had not. These are the times we need to make a change.

Think about how you would like to respond to the pressure you are getting.

When you have a clear idea about how you would like to respond to the pressure to eat more than you would like, think about a time you have been able to respond to anyone with assertiveness, about anything. It could be a time when you were young, or a time at work.

Think of exactly where you were and how you felt. While feeling powerful in this state that was able to respond assertively, think of a name for this part of you, maybe 'Assertive' or 'Powerful' or something like that. Speak directly to this part of you on the inside with the question, 'Assertive', are you willing to come out and help me when people try to pressure me about food?"

This is making a deal with this part of you that it will be there to help you when you need it. Parts like to help, and it will be able to as long a Vaded state is not still jumping out in front of it.

If you cannot find a part of yourself that has ever been assertive in the way you would like to respond, think of how someone you admire would be able to respond. Define exactly how they would respond, then get a name for this part of you that has the ability to define this assertive behavior, the part that is defining it. Then say directly to this part, "Assertive', since you have such a good understanding of assertiveness, even though you have not been assertive in the past would you be the assertive part for me and respond to the pressure in the way you know is right?"

We have covered the first two steps, checking for and healing a Vaded state, and responding to pressure. It is important that these steps are finished before going to the third step.

Now we can learn how to move from the habit of eating things that are bad for us to the habit of eating things we really want to eat. We accomplish this by making sure we have a Resource State out that is strong enough to demand the body take in only the right foods.

Step 3: How to make sure a Resource State is out that is strong enough to demand the body eat the right foods.

Think about something you would never do. It can be anything, rob a bank, kill someone, eat a spider, anything. Now think about someone standing in front of you who is trying to talk you into doing this thing. The part of you that can say, 'No (I would never do that)' is coming out now. Now that your "NO" state is out get a name for it. What name fits you when you are in this state?

Call this part by the name you have given it, and ask it if it is willing to come out when you are tempted to eat something that you prefer not to. If this state is named 'NO' have it to have an internal hand shake with the part of you that understands what healthy eating is, so it will be able to be called out exactly when it is needed to say NO.

Now, think about making a decision about a food that would have been tempting in the past. It may still be tempting, but now you have your 'NO' state there ready to be firm, to say 'no way'.

It is important to recognize the part that also wants to eat. See it as a good part of you that needs something, so try to give it something that will help it feel attended to. All our parts are important and they should feel able to respect each other and compromise. If the part that wants to eat feels respected and if it gets something it will cooperate. Parts should never feel neglected or forced. We want peace on the inside.

Remember, this 'No' state will need to have good communication with a state that knows the best foods for the body, and there will appropriately be times of compromise when special foods are eaten in moderation.

So the three steps to eat what we want to eat are:

1. Make sure a Vaded state is not involved in our eating and if it is resolve it,
2. Learn how to respond to pressure, and
3. Learn how to be empowered to break habits of eating the wrong types of food.

Breaking a habit may also involve feeling physical withdrawals during the time we are breaking the habit. In order to lessen these we can decide to move gradually into our new routine. Anything is possible as long as our states are in agreement. Why not help the body to be as comfortable as possible as we move to our preferred eating habits.

For example, if you are moving from drinking full cream milk or from 2% milk to skim milk you could gradually move to lower fat milk. If I wanted to break my coffee habit I could drink less each day until it is easy to stop. This kind of gradual reduction is possible when a Vaded state is not there with its bad feelings forcing us to escape with food. When the Vaded states have been helped into a Normal state we are free to work on whatever we want. Achieving the weight you want may not be easy, and your goals need to be reasonable, but you do have power to heal and change.

> **Anything is possible as long as your states are in agreement. You do have power to heal and change.**

Chapter 9: Sleep

We spend an amazing amount of our life sleeping. Some of us would like to spend more time sleeping, and some of us would like to spend less. We would probably all like to get a good sleep and feel ready to go when we wake up.

Resource States have a lot to do with sleep. While we all have a Resource State that would like to shut down and rest, some people have Resource States that feel compelled to think, but feel they have not had enough opportunity during the day to figure out problems, or to focus on parts of the body or other issues. Before we look at Resource State issues with sleep let's look at some of the things we know about sleep.

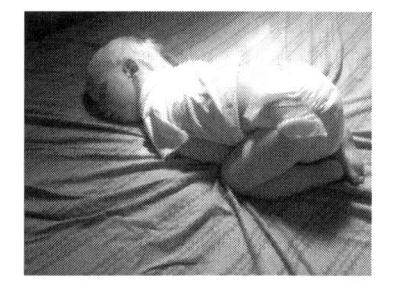

There are four stages of sleep plus REM. Most adults generally sleep in a circadian rhythm; that is in 90 minute cycles. Once we go to sleep we initially go into stage I sleep, then stage II, stage III, stage IV, and REM. The different stages can be distinguished by different brainwave patterns so a sleep technician can observe an EEG readout and determine what sleep stage a person is in.

Figure 1: Stages of Sleep as shown on an EEG, source: http://www.sleepdex.org/stages.htm

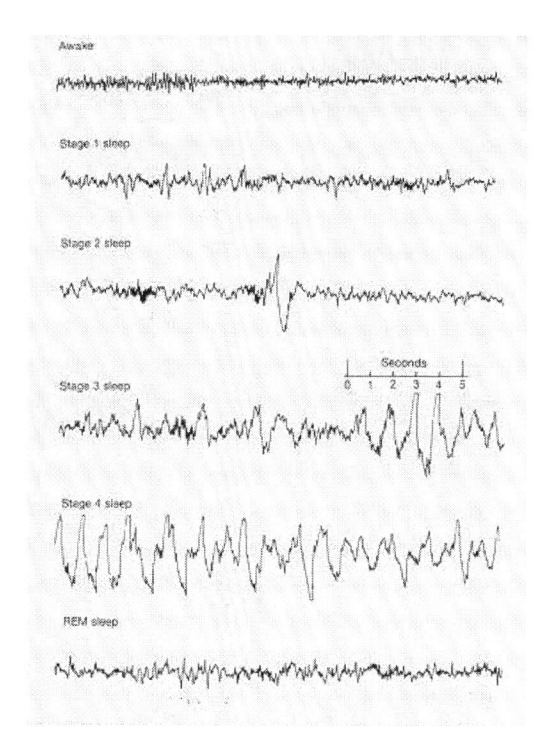

We do not go into every stage of sleep during every cycle. Most adults get stage IV sleep only during the first 90 minutes. Occasionally they will get some in the next 90 minutes cycle but normally not after that. Stage IV sleep is important because it helps determine how well we will perform during the next day. It is our deepest state of sleep.

Our bodies become accustomed to the time we go to bed. That means if we normally go to bed at 10:30 PM are stage IV sleep normally occurs before midnight. If we disrupt our normal pattern and go to bed later, after midnight, we will not get our normal stage IV sleep time for that night. Therefore, we will probably not accomplish as well the next day as we otherwise would. If we want to study for a test it is better to do that by getting up early in the morning, rather than studying late at night so we will not miss out on our stage IV sleep.

In the morning we tend to have more REM time; that is dreamtime. If we miss out on REM sleep we may feel a bit more anxious during the day but our ability level is not much affected. Studies have been done where individuals are kept from having REM time during sleep. In other words they are kept from dreaming.

Even though we do not remember many of our dreams we do all dream. An EEG makes it possible to see when dreamtime sleep begins, so it is possible to wake a person each time they begin to dream. By doing this is possible to eliminate dreams during sleep. After having one night of no dreams a person can expect to feel a bit more anxious the next day. After having two nights with no rem time the anxiety increases. After a few nights of not being able to dream a person will get highly anxious and will begin hallucinating. It appears that our dreams help reduce our anxiety. It appears that they are symbolic representations of anxiety that help 'let the steam' out.

It is interesting that our body is actually paralysed while we are dreaming. The only part of our body that normally moves while we are dreaming is our eyes. A person who is dreaming will normally be still except their eyes which will be moving back and forth under the closed eyelids. You can see the eyes moving under the eyelids. That is why dreamtime is called REM, rapid eye movement.

Stage I is the lightest level of sleep. At night when we first enter into sleep, stage I is the first stage we enter. It is interesting that when we are in stage I sleep we do not think we are asleep. When a sleep technician wakes a person from stage I sleep with the question, "Are you asleep?" the person will normally respond, "No, I was just thinking."

You don't even have to have an EEG to do this experiment. While they are going to sleep, you can have a friend or partner very quietly repeat a single digit number each time you say it. For example, when the person who is going to sleep agrees to repeat a single digit number quietly, after that person has been quiet for one minute you can say the number, 2, low and quietly. The person will repeat quietly, 2. After 60 more seconds you say another number such as 4. The person attempting to go to sleep may repeat quietly, 4. For a few minutes you continue this process with numbers such as, 1, 6, 3, 9, randomly so that the person only has to repeat quietly a one digit number. When the person who's going to sleep fails to repeat a number during a couple of 60 second cycles, you know they have entered into stage I sleep. At that point you can ask the person, "Are you asleep?" Their reply will normally be, "No, I was just thinking."

Stage I sleep is a time when our mind continues to process information, and we continue to try to figure out our problems even though we are asleep. This process can continue also into stage II sleep. Because of this, it is possible for a person to have actually gotten quite a few minutes or hours of sleep when they say I did not sleep at all. To them, they were just thinking.

The difference between sleep and being awake is distinguished by a lack of awareness to stimuli around the person. It is not distinguished by whether or not we are thinking. It is therefore important not to give up too quickly when attempting to go to sleep, because in reality you may already be asleep while you are thinking.

It is much better to enter into sleep from a deep relaxation than from nervous thought. It is possible to sleep the whole night and wake up feeling like you have not received much rest. And you probably haven't.

Before we talk about how our Resource States can help us get more and deeper sleep it is important to know some practical aspects of improving sleep. Here are some techniques that can help us get better sleep.

Common techniques for better sleep

- Get up in the morning at the right time. Don't sleep in too late.
- If you want to sleep through the night, don't sleep during the day.
- Do not watch TV, read, or surf the Internet after you get into bed.
- As much as possible, go to bed at the same time each night.
- Do not consume caffeine or apples for a number of hours before going to bed.
- Do not do exercise for number of hours before going to bed.
- If you do not feel sleepy don't go to bed until you do, but make sure you still get up in the morning at the same time.
- Don't go to bed feeling lazy because you have not attended to a task you should have. It there is something you need to do, do it or do it at least until you are sleepy.

Remember, when you attend to these things your sleep pattern will not change immediately. It is normally at least one week before a sleep pattern shows real evidence of change, and that usually happens only if you are able to stick strictly to your new routine. If you are already doing these things, and you get your Resource States working together for better sleep then sleep patterns may change even during the first night. It is important to tend to these common techniques for better sleep first so they do not interfere with the good work you do to make sure that your Resource States are working together.

> **Often people get their internal sleep time clock set to the wrong time and it is like they are suffering from jet lag.**

Get up in the morning at the right time
In order to go to sleep when we want to at night we need to wake up in the morning at a time that would normally make us tired at the time we went to sleep. For example, if we want to go to sleep at 10:30 PM and we feel like we need eight hours of sleep we should set our alarm for 6:30 AM, even if we went to bed or went to sleep at 2 AM. If we sleep late into the morning it can keep us from being sleepy at the time that we want to go to sleep.

An example of this is getting over jet lag. After making a long international air flight we may find ourselves in a place where 11 clock AM is actually 6:00 AM in the place that we just travelled from. If we continue to allow ourselves to sleep until 11:00 AM we will never become tired at the time we want to go to sleep. Therefore, we have to set our alarms for 6 AM and make sure we get up at that time, and continue to do that, in order to reset our body's clock to the times we want to sleep.

Often people get their internal sleep time clock set to the wrong time and it is like they are suffering from jet lag. It is not unusual for teenagers, during school holidays, to get in the practice of staying up late and sleeping late. Usually it takes them a while to reset their body's internal clock when they go back to school.

Even though it may be hard to continue to get up at the right time, it is the only way we will have a chance to learn to go to sleep at the right time.

If you want to sleep through the night, don't sleep during the day

I can hear you say, I have to sleep during the day because I'm not sleeping at night. People who have to work during the day, especially people who are working outside and do not have an opportunity to sleep during the day sleep better at night.

It is common for people who are retired or the people who spend a lot of time at home to get into the habit of watching TV or reading and taking a nap, often falling asleep in the middle of the TV or during their reading time. This can be very comfortable and there's not anything wrong with it as long as you're happy not to sleep much at night. Often these people who tend to nap during the day, (and remember stage I sleep is thinking and many people who are in stage one do not realise they are sleeping,) are the same people who complain about not being able to sleep at night.

If you want to sleep at night keep busy during the day. If you feel tired or sleepy do something physical to get your blood moving. Staying alert until the time you go to bed increases the body's ability to attain a quick and restful sleep.

It is not rocket science. If you do not eat you get hungry, and if you do not sleep during the day you are more likely to be sleepy when it is time for bed.

Do not watch TV, read, or surf the Internet after you go to bed

We are creatures of habit. If we get used to watching TV, reading, or surfing the Internet after we go to bed we will learn to expect these activities. We can easily get to the point where bed is seen as a place to watch TV, read, or surf the net rather than a place to sleep. Resource States that do those activities will learn to come into the conscious to do them at bed time.

If we go to bed when we are tired and do none of those activities after going to bed we can build up the habit that bed is a place to sleep. This habit can help us go to sleep more quickly. Our sleep confidence builds as does our ability to get to sleep quickly.

As much as possible, go to bed at the same time each night

Our bodies have an internal clock. We become used to going to sleep at a certain time. We are lucky when we are able to continue to go to sleep at the same time. There will always be times we want to stay up for something, but, generally, it is important for our bodies to be trained that a specific time at night is our sleep time.

Jet lag is not only something that affects international travellers. The same difficulty in struggling with the internal clock is experienced by shift workers, who may have to work at night through the week and then attempt to sleep at night during weekend days. This can be very difficult to do.

By going to bed at the same time each night our bodies learn the time of day that stage IV sleep is to be experienced, during the first 90 minutes of sleep. If we go to bed later we will miss that night's stage IV sleep. Our stage IV sleep assists us in functioning better during the day and helps us feel more rested, so it is important to have a specified 'sleep time'.

Do not consume caffeine or apples for a number of hours before going to bed

I have met a number of people who say that caffeine does not affect them. Some of them appear to be right. They can have a coffee late at night before they go to bed and still sleep. Most of them appear to be wrong.

Caffeine affects most people and interrupts sleep. Some people cannot have caffeine any time after midday without their sleep being interrupted. They may not be able to go to sleep when they want to, or if they are able to go to sleep it may not be a deep and restful sleep that they would otherwise have had the opportunity to get.

Apples are a great food, and they're very healthy. It is also true that eating an apple will keep you awake. Some people eat apples to stay awake while driving. It is better not to have an apple for a few hours before you are ready to go to sleep.

Do not do exercise for a number of hours before going to bed

Exercise gets the blood moving and heart rate going. If you are feeling tired or sleepy during the day exercise is a good way to wake up and feel alert. It is not a good thing to do in the immediate hours before going to bed.

Exercise during the day is good for sleep. When the body has become physically tired, and when the mind knows that things have been accomplished it is easier to sleep. Just make sure the exercise comes well before sleep, with the exception of sexual exercise. Many people find after a sexual climax that it is easy to go to sleep.

If you do not feel sleepy don't go to bed until you do, but make sure you still get up in the morning at the right time

I mentioned earlier that habit is an important aspect of good sleep. It is important not to get into the habit of lying in bed without sleeping. It is important to get into the habit of going to sleep rather quickly after going to bed. Therefore, it's best not to go to bed until you feel sleepy.

You can read, watch TV, do some work, or talk to a friend before you go to bed. When you feel sleepy, and it is at least your sleep time then it is the time to go to bed. For example, if you feel sleepy at 7 PM and you want 11 PM to be your sleep time you would not go to bed, and if it is 11 PM and you do not feel sleepy then don't go to bed, then at 11:30 if you become sleepy then go to bed.

You may find that you do not feel sleepy until 1 AM. That is okay. Stay up until you feel sleepy, but make sure that if 7 AM is the time that you choose to normally wake up to get up at 7 AM. Don't sleep during the day, and your body will most likely begin to tell you what time it needs to sleep.

Don't go to bed feeling lazy

A common reason people have difficulty falling asleep is because they feel they have not done what they need to get done during the day. Often one of the things they feel they need to get done is planning.

Before you go to bed ask yourself if there's anything you really need to do before going to sleep. If there is, then make an attempt to get it done. It may be that while making the attempt to get it done you will become very sleepy, then you can make an agreement with yourself to finish up tomorrow and sleep tonight.

Make sure you have all the planning you need to do finished before you go to bed. Sit at a table, in a comfortable chair, or walk and spend time planning for the next day or for your future. Your planning Resource State needs to feel like it has had time to work on its plans. You will be able to tell when the Resource State that can sleep is ready to take over.

If you go to bed feeling lazy there may be a feeling of, "Not having a right," to sleep. You are much more likely to quickly enter into a restful and deep sleep if you have given time to your other Resource States to finish what they need to do during the day. This will always be a compromise between the state that needs to sleep and the states that want to get things done and we will talk about this in the next section.

Resource State techniques for better sleep

In the last section we have already started talking about the interplay of Resource States and sleep. Some people have tried what they thought was everything (above) and they were still not able to sleep. They may feel tired during the day and experience low levels of energy because their body is not getting the sleep that it needs.

Resource State techniques for better sleep are very powerful and they work best if you are already attending to most, or all, of the common techniques for better sleep covered above. I recommend that you follow as many of the above techniques as possible for a minimum of one week before using these powerful Resource State techniques.

Sleep is a very natural process. When we are hungry we eat, when we are thirsty we drank, and when we are sleepy it is natural to sleep. Sleep happens by itself unless something gets in the way. If we clear the way for sleep it will happen.

We all have a state that is tired. It exists to recharge our body with sleep. Sometimes that state is frustrated by other states hogging the mind or the body. We all sometimes feel that frustration. Our sleep state is wanting to help us get a good night's rest. It just needs permission from our other states to have that time for sleep.

There are 2 Resource State dynamics they can move us from poorer sleep to better sleep.

1. All Resource States need to make sure that the sleep state has permission to use the time in bed for sleeping, and

2. Resource States that have carried fear need to learn empowerment so we can have peace when we lay down to sleep.

Giving permission for the sleeping Resource State to sleep

We are always in a Resource State. If you are having trouble getting to sleep you are in a Resource State. If you are sleeping you are in a Resource State. If you want to sleep it is important for you to be in the Resource State that sleeps, therefore it is important for that state to have permission to do what it does.

If your mind is thinking about something else and that is keeping you from being able to sleep you are in a Resource State that has a need to figure something out and it is forcing itself out in front of the state that would like to sleep.

Ask yourself, what is it that I need to plan, to figure out, or to learn? Respectfully, tell that part of you that has a need to plan, to figure out, or to learn that you want to make sure that it gets the time to do that. Tell that part of yourself that you are glad that it is there to help you and that you will give it a set amount of time in the morning, or even before you go to bed to do what it needs to do, and also tell this part of yourself that it will be able to do this best with a rested body.

You need to respect this part of you that has a need to plan, figure out, or learn, and you need to tell it that it is important, and that the Resource State that sleeps is also important. Get a compromise between the part of you that is tired and wants to sleep, and the other part about the time they will each get and then get an internal handshake on the deal they have made. The more directly you can do this process the better it works. Here's an example.

Getting to know your sleep state

It is important to get to know a state that you have that can sleep. Think about a time when you have really been able to let go and relax. It may have been when you were in a hot bath, it may have been when you were laying on the beach, or it may have been when you were so tired you could not do anything but relax. Think about what it feels like for the body to release muscles, to let go, and to allow the mind to drift. Think about what it feels like for the body to be totally supported by the chair, by a beach, in the bath, or on the bed, with zero effort. While feeling this state, ask yourself what this state can be called. Let's say the answer is, "Deep."

Speak directly to Deep on the inside saying, "Thank you for helping me rest and recharge my system. I need you and you are important to me. When given the chance, will you help me rest deeply and get the sleep that I need? Will you be available to me to do what you do best, rest and sleep when I am in bed? I will get permission from other parts so you can do what you do best."

Getting to know this part of you and getting an agreement from this part of you to help you when it is given the opportunity is important. It is always good to bring our resources to our needs.

Getting permission

After going to bed if you find that you are not able to sleep because of thinking, get up, go to a comfortable chair, sit down and internally address this part of you that was thinking.

"Part, I respect you and I need you and I'm glad that you're there. What you do is important to me. What term or name can I call you? (Once you get a name for this part call it directly by name. For this example let's assume the name is, "Planner.") "Planner, I want to give you 10 minutes right now to help you plan. If that is not enough time I want to give you another 30 minutes in the morning from 7:30 AM to 8 AM. It is important that you plan, and it is also important that the body sleeps. Is it okay with you for me to go back to bed in 10 minutes, after you have some time, and for my sleep state (Deep) to be able to help the body so I can get a good night's sleep? Will you please directly on the inside give a message to 'Deep' that you will allow Deep to rest and sleep?" Encourage an internal respectful handshake between these two important parts.

Getting the states to respect and communicate directly together allows each state to know how important they both are. When you go back to bed, invite sleep to have the body, making sure that it has permission from all states, without any noise in the head.

Helping states move from fear to peace

It is most often the case that the above process of planning is all that is needed to help the person enter into the sleep state. Occasionally though a Vaded state will feel fear and that can interfere with the sleep state from coming out. If this is the case the techniques in Chapter 5 can help soothe the Vaded state so that the sleep state can have permission to come out and be given time to allow the body to rest and drift.

If fear is experienced when attempting to go to sleep use the helping hand that was charged in Chapter 5 to soothe the fearful part. At the same time permission can be given for the sleep state to have the body so that the body can sink more deeply into the mattress, can rest, and can drift.

When sleeping, it is important to allow the body to be in a position that does not put strain on muscles or on the back. Find a comfortable position and invite the sleep state to do what it does best. Suggest to the sleep state to keep the body in a position that will be good for the back and body.

Here is an example of moving into the right Resource State for sleep after all preparation is made. You lie down and find that, although tired and sleepy you are not going to sleep. You send an inner message of thank you to the Resource State that has come to the surface and remind it that now is the time for the sleep Resource State to do what it does best, release, just be, and have permission to move toward drifting. Move the body so that it can lie restfully and send the message for your 'Deep' sleep state to have the night. Knowing what this state feels like helps as the body releases with permission for the night.

Resource States during sleep

I have found that Resource States often use dreams. When I am working with a client and I speak with a Resource State that enjoys playing I often suggest it can come out and play when the client has an opportunity to play, and it can also play in the dreams. Afterward clients often report that their dreams become more playful.

I've also found that the anxiety or fear felt in dreams are a direct reflection of the anxiety or fear felt by Resource States. If I talk to a client about a dream and bring out the fear that they felt in the dream we can often bridge back to where this fear came from in the client's life. Then the Resource State can learn that the fear it has held onto is a figment from the past and has no power in the present. It is a way of moving a Vaded state to a Normal state.

Another interesting thing about dreams is it seems that the different major roles in the dreams are played by different Resource States. For example, if we dream about two people having an argument one of the people in that argument is actually one of our Resource States, and the other person in the argument is another Resource State. They are symbolic representations of each Resource State they represent. That way, both Resource States get to release in the dream some level of their anxieties.

This makes sense because our mind is creating each person in the dream. It makes sense that our mind would not create a person unless there was a reason for that person to be created, unless there was a payoff to us. Nothing happens for no reason. The mind is an amazing thing.

Remember, sleep is natural. All animals sleep. It is OK for sleep to be different during different nights. Sleep will naturally happen and all it needs is internal permission. It is OK if our sleep is different from the norm. It is just important to have energy during the day.

Chapter 10: Competition

There are two types of competition. There is the loving to play a game or sport and wanting to win, but being able to be happy with whoever wins. This is the good kind of competition, where we challenge ourselves against another person (or ourselves) and enjoy competing. If we win it may feel nice, and if they win it feels like we had a good competition and there may even be some enjoyment that the other person gets a win.

Then there is the other kind of competition. It is very different. It is not enjoying the game or the sport, but feeling a need to be as good as someone else, or better. If we lose this kind of competition we have a bad feeling, and it is a bad feeling that causes us to want to compete in this way. This kind of competition comes from an insecurity.

While it is great to enjoy the good kind of competition, if we feel this insecure 'have to' kind of competition it is better to change, so we can be free just to enjoy and be who we are. That may sound funny, being free to be who we are, being related to competition. But in truth we often buy things we don't want, we spend time and money on things that we really don't care about, we may dress up in a way that we really don't like, just to feel good enough. This is being out of control and not being who we really are.

We might meet a person who seems really comfortable in their own skin, who seems authentic, and who gives a sense that they are not competing. They are just being who they really are. These people tend to give us calm. They share their calm with us. They don't care if their car is the right brand, or the latest model. They may have a new nice car because they enjoy driving it, but it will not be because they need the esteem of the car, or need to compete.

Wouldn't it be nice to buy the things that give us joy, regardless of what other people think? Right now, if you are one of the people who has a need to compete that last sentence may be threatening to you. It might seem threatening to you to wear clothes that are a common brand, just because you like them.

If you feel driven in life you may suffer from a need to compete. It is actually pretty simple where this comes from. It comes from a Vaded state, sometimes more than one. **The person who feels a need to compete to be okay has a Resource State that is seeking love or acceptance.** It is almost always a child state that has experienced a feeling of rejection or neglect, a state that has not received unconditional love.

What needs to happen?

Moving from being competitive to just feeling okay can be threatening to some. There is a sense of "I have to compete" and to think about not competing can bring out

> **The person who feels a need to compete to be okay has a Resource State that is seeking love or acceptance.**

the fear of not being okay. There may be the feeling of, "If I don't excel, I won't be good enough."

There can also be a pride of accomplishment brought about by the neurotic 'over effort'. Probably some of the most famous people in history have been compelled to work almost all the time. They did not have well rounded lives, which would mean spending time enjoying leisure and friends the way more healthy people do. Some people may decide that they want to keep their neurotic competiveness because they can't picture themselves being more normal. They may even have learned to put normal people down, to criticize them. Some over-competitors have learned to accept themselves, and the amount of extreme effort they make in living by telling themselves that to be normal with a well-rounded life is to be not good enough.

This is sad. People with well-rounded lives also make great contributions to the world. They just feel more relaxed while doing it. Obviously, it is for each person to decide the type of life that is wanted. But, wouldn't it be nice if that decision was made while feeling in control?

The problem with negative competitiveness is that the person caught in that cycle is out of control. They do not have a choice. They have to compete. They are competing to escape the bad feelings they would have if they did not compete. It is not a joy that drives them, it is a fear.

This is the vision, to be free to make our own decisions about the work we want to do, about the things we want to buy, and about the kinds of competition we want to enjoy. The vision is to be able to be relaxed while resting, to be able to go on holiday and enjoy the place that we are in while relaxing. The vision is to be able to see something nice that someone else has, and feel happy that they have it, and feel no need to match or excel it.

This vision is not that difficult to bring to reality. It is the anxiety that is felt immediately before competitive behavior that makes a person feel out of control. It is the tender spot in our psyche, the Vaded Resource State that compels us to compete. This is the state that needs healing.

In order to heal the Vaded state that compels anxiety driven competition we must first locate it and experience its feelings. This is not hard to do. All you have to do is to think of not competing. If you compete by buying designer clothes that you really do not want, think about not buying any of these clothes. It won't be long until you feel anxiety. The more anxiety you feel, the more upset you feel, the clearer it is that the right Resource State is coming out.

When you are experiencing this negative feeling, this real need to compete, then the right Resource State is out. At this time you can use the techniques described in Chapter 5, "Healing the Vaded state." Each time you feel this anxiety, this being compelled to work, to buy, to feel okay, use the techniques from that chapter, use the nurturing hand that you have carefully prepared. You will find that as you bring the helping hand to the part of the body associated with the Vaded state these feelings of anxiety will lessen and disappear.

You will find that you will gain the ability to make up your own mind about what you want to buy and do. You will find that you will be able to feel positive about what others can do and about what they have, and this will help your relationships. You will be a more enjoyable friend.

Think about people who are able to rejoice about your accomplishments, people who do not compete with you, and people who just appreciate you. These people probably make you feel comfortable, and they help others to feel comfortable. Wouldn't it be nice to be one of these people? This is what you can be.

Just remember, when you begin feeling that sense of not being okay, possibly a little panic, a feeling of being little or small, use the techniques in the section on healing Vaded states. Bring your helping hand to that part of the body that most feels the anxiety, and use the techniques as described. It is very important that you read that section carefully and properly prepare your helping hand with one of your nurturing Resource States so that you will be prepared when the time comes.

Chapter 11: Addictions

All psychological addictions have in common the need to escape from a Vaded state.

What is a Psychological Addiction?

We can think of a psychological addiction as the same as having an addictive personality, and this means there is a need to escape from bad feelings into the addictive behavior. A person has the potential of having an addictive personality if they have a Vaded state that occasionally comes to the surface with its bad feelings. All Vaded states do not cause addictions, but all psychological addictions are caused by Vaded states.

Therefore, all psychological addictions need the Vaded state to become a Normal state. Addictions vary somewhat in terms of how the addiction is able to give relief from the bad feelings. For example drugs physically can block states from coming to the surface so they chemically give relief from the upset state, while many other additions provide a zoned out, safe place, away from the Vaded state. These include gambling, obsessive compulsive disorder, compulsive spending, compulsive eating or smoking, workaholism, and others. Even self-harming behavior can be an addiction where it seems preferable to zone out into harming behavior rather than to feel the anxiety of a Vaded state.

The good news is, Vaded states can become Normal states. It is helpful to understand more about specific types of addictions, but the resolution to all addictions is the resolution of the Vaded state. Chapter 5, on healing Vaded states, and this chapter on Addictions go hand in hand. There are differences in when to use the techniques on healing states and they will be covered.

Addictions: Drug addiction

Every time someone uses a drug, even an illicit drug, it doesn't mean they are necessarily psychologically addicted. As mentioned earlier, it is possible to have a physiological addiction, like many people's addiction to drinking coffee or many people's addiction to eating fatty foods, without having a psychological addiction.

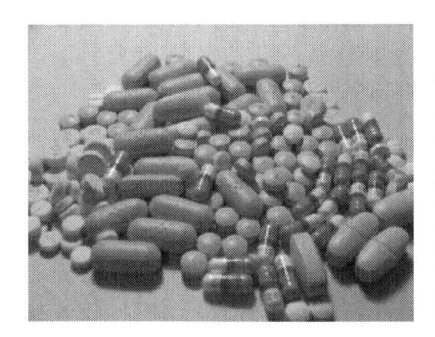

Here is how drug addiction works. Some drugs block Resource States chemically from coming to the surface. This is how antidepressants work, by blocking Resource States that have bad feelings. An antidepressant is not doing therapy, it is chemically blocking Resource States from coming to the surface. When antidepressants are taken the unhappy Resource States are still there, but they are not able to come to the surface as easily. This can help the person feel better although it does not solve the problem. Still, there are times when antidepressants are appropriate, and sometimes when Resource States having bad feelings are blocked for a period of time other Resource States may strengthen and be able to stay strong when the antidepressants are no longer taken.

Drugs can do the same thing. Many people may experiment with drugs without becoming addicted, but if a person has a Vaded state that comes to the surface with bad feelings, and that person finds a drug that blocks those bad feelings then the 'drug of choice' has been found.

It is very difficult for the person not to continue to return to their 'drug of choice' over and over again to continue to have the relief that it provides. It feels tremendously better being free of the bad feelings that the Vaded state carries. There is little wonder that individuals have such a hard time getting off of a drug that blocks these bad feelings. If they attempt to stop using the drug, they often have to also contend with a physiological addiction that they have built while taking the drug, as well as having to contend with the psychological effects of the troubled Vaded state returning with its bad feelings. It can be overwhelming for the person, so they often find it easier to return to the drug.

It is the psychological addiction that causes the drug user to often return to the drug even after they have gone through the withdrawal symptoms of a physiological addiction. The psychological addiction is often more difficult to handle than the physiological addiction.

Dealing with the psychological aspects of drug dependency

There is some good news in this, because the psychological addiction can be attended to. If the Vaded state that caused the addiction in the first place is able to get the nurturance, support, and relief that it needs then it will no longer require the drug of choice to block its bad feelings. This means that the only addiction the drug addict has to contend with is a physiological addiction, if there is one.

It is a bit tricky to help the Vaded state of someone who is abusing drugs, because if they have found their drug of choice it is blocking the state that needs help. A Vaded state cannot be helped if it cannot come out. It cannot come out if a drug is blocking it. Therefore, the only way to break the psychological addiction is to stop taking the drug that is blocking the Vaded state from coming to the surface.

Once the drug is no longer taken, it will not be long before the Vaded state comes to the surface carrying with it its bad feelings.

It is very important for the person who has a drug addiction to prepare well, making sure they have found a helping state (Chapter 5) and grounded it into the helping hand. Their helping state needs to be associated with their helping hand so that it will be ready to alleviate the negative feelings as soon as they come out.

The love and support the helping state transmits to the Vaded state help heal the Vaded state. The person using this technique needs to take plenty of time making sure they feel the love and nurturance of their helping state and that they feel this love and nurturance grounded in their helping hand. Preparation is the key.

In essence, what is happening is they are using their internal resources. They're using a part of them that would like to help in order to bring support, understanding, and nurturance for the part of them that desperately needs help, so that part can feel settled, secure, and supported.

Resource State steps to breaking a psychological drug dependency addiction are:

1. Prepare carefully using the techniques in the chapter, 'Healing the Vaded state.' Practice the procedures over and over again until you are totally comfortable with them.
2. Become ready to deal with any bad feelings that may be experienced when the drug is not going to be used any longer.
3. Stop taking the drug.
4. As negative emotions come to the surface use the charged helping hand to bring peace and support to the child Resource State that has carried these negative emotions. Make sure the loving hug, pressing in with the hand, is experienced and felt.
5. Continue this process of sending love and support to the Resource State that feels anxiety until there are no physiological or psychological demands for the drug, then you are free of the pull for the drug. You will no longer have a need for it to block anything.

> **We all have Resource States that hold childhood memories that our adult states do not have access to.**

Dealing with the physical sensations

Resource State techniques can also help deal with the aspects of physiological addiction. One should not attempt to break a drug habit without attending to the psychological aspects of addiction, but as those are being dealt with the physical pain of stopping something that the body has become used to can be challenging.

We can use techniques that will make it easier. In order to make it easier we need to feel less physical pain. A good thing about Resource States is that one state is capable of feeling a pain that another state does not experience. Hypnotherapists use this technique often. Some dentists use hypnosis to assist their patients to have drilling and extractions while they experience no pain.

Here is how the technique works. It is not unusual for a person to drive for 10 or 15 minutes and then realize that they have no memory of having driven for that period of time. As explained earlier, this is an example of one Resource State not communicating with another Resource State. The Resource State that drove the 10 or 15 minutes was capable of driving and was capable of thinking, but when the person changed Resource States they changed into a state that was not communicating with the previous state. Therefore, the second state had no memory of the driving for the past 10 or 15 minutes. This ability for Resource States to be unaware of what other Resource States are experiencing is common for us all. It is natural.

We all have Resource States that hold childhood memories that our adult states do not have access to. This means we have

Resource States that do not communicate with each other. This can be helpful when we want the conscious Resource State to be unaware of a pain or sensation. If an underlying Resource State is willing to experience the pain so that the conscious state does not have to. The person will not consciously experience pain even though an underlying Resource State does.

This is how hypnotherapy can allow a person to be operated on without feeling any pain. An underlying state that is not out and conscious experiences the pain and it is not communicating with the conscious surface state that is out. Therefore, the surface state, the state that is conscious is not aware of the pain. This is good for the surface state but not really that good for the underlying state. If an underlying state is asked to experience pain so that the conscious surface state does not have to it should be done with the permission of the underlying state. Here is how to do this.

Set down in a comfortable chair in a quiet place. Close your eyes and give yourself some time to relax and focus, and while you do this be aware of the sensations that you do not want to experience as you come off the drug. It is OK, possibly preferable, if you experience some fear about this.

While you are thinking about this with an amount of fear or trepidation ask this part of yourself that fears the physical withdrawal what would be a good name for it. It is important for it to be able to name itself, but let's say it chooses the name, 'Afraid'. Allow Afraid to be honest and say internally, "I am afraid and I need some help from a brave, underlying state that would be willing to take some of the sensations that will come from me stopping the use of the drug. I would like this brave and courageous state to please get this message so when the sensations come I will be able to get off the drug. This would be a great thing that you do for me and I will be very thankful."

You don't have to say those words exactly, but it is important for you to ask that question and send that message without trying to get a reply. When you ask for this help, say your words out loud. Just send it down. What you are after is a Resource State that the conscious state is not highly connected to, because when that state experiences a sensation the surface states will not have to. It is also important to say one more thing to this underlying state that you are sending the message to. "I will ask a nurturing Resource State to come and help you deal with the sensations that you experience. This Resource State will also be grateful to you, and it will give you love." By letting the underlying state know this, you are helping to make it easier both for the state to deal with the sensations, and for it to be willing to volunteer.

While still sitting with your eyes closed you can stop sending messages to the underlying state. It is good to send one final thank you, but do not try to get a reply because it is to your advantage not to be able to hear the underlying state. You do not want the communication running from that underlying state to the conscious state, because you do not want to feel what it feels.

Next, still while sitting quietly and focused, send a clear message to your nurturing state, the one that can give safety and support by using your charged, helping hand. Again speak out loud to it. Say something like. "I have asked for a brave underlying state to take on some sensations so I don't have to feel them. Please do what you do best. Please help this state by sharing your safety and support with it. I very much appreciate all the help you provide. I am lucky to have you."

This is the preparation you need to make it physically easier to stop taking the drug. Now, we can focus on motivation.

This is the same technique as discussed in the section on weight loss. You need to find a state that can say no. In order to do this, think about anything that you know you would never, ever do. When you think of this thing that you know you would never do think about how strongly you would refuse, then ask yourself, "What can I call this part of me that can vehemently say, 'NO'?" Allow it to name itself, but it may choose a name like No or Strong. Then, calling this part by its name, ask it if during any temptation it will be willing to come out and help you by using its ability to say, "No, no I will not do that." When you get a commitment from this strong part that is capable of saying no this will help empower you to resist the drug. Use this only when you are already attending to the Psychological and Physiological demands for the drug. It is better to work with a team than to rely on a single state.

There are three points here to help you become empowered:
>Make sure the first thing you do is attend to the psychological issues (the Vaded state) of the addiction since these are the strongest, and you will need to continue dealing with these throughout the process,
>
>Get help from underlying Resource States to deal with the physical sensations, and

Get help from a strong part of you that is able to say an emphatic, "No."

Also use any other help available. Make it as easy for yourself as possible. If it is easier to taper off slowly then do that, unless that is ill-advised.

Helping Confused Resource States
There is a further thing that can happen with individuals who have been using a drug for some period of time in order to block the bad feelings of a Vaded state. The drug may block not only the state that has the bad feelings, but may also block other states as well. While the person is using the drug these states are not an active part of the family of states, and are not able to carry out their normal roles. Therefore, other Resource States take up the slack. They take over roles that the states that are being blocked by the drug previously had. Therefore, once the drug is no longer used there may be confusion among states in terms of which states will be coming out to help the person. I will give you an example.

Let's say Eve has a problem with alcohol. Before she started using alcohol she had a sensitive and caring state that would talk to her mother and would talk to other close friends and relatives. We can call this state, 'Kind'. When Eve used alcohol her state, Kind, was blocked along with the child state that was vaded. Therefore, Eve no longer experienced either the Vaded child state or her state, Kind, as long as she was using alcohol.

She still had to communicate with her mother and other close friends and relatives so an articulate, but less caring state took over this activity. We can call the state, 'Salesperson.' Salesperson was very good at communicating and in her own way was very charming, although not as sensitive as Kind.

When Eve stopped using alcohol Kind was available to her again, as was Salesperson. This caused Resource State confusion for Eve. Two states were available for the same job. This Resource State confusion can result in Conflicted states. Kind and Salesperson both want to come out at the same time and unless they can compromise conflict may be the result.

If a person who has been addicted to a drug experiences this Resource State confusion and conflict then the techniques in the chapter, Achieving Respect among Our States, should be used. It is important for Resource States to be able to compromise so they can be good internal family members. This Resource State confusion is not directly associated with the drug use. Therefore, if it is not attended to it does not mean that the person will have a desire to return to the drug. But it does mean that the person may not be settled on the inside. There needs to be a rebalancing of states following the cessation of a drug addiction and this will happen sooner or later.

Here is an example of what Eve could do to help her confused and Conflicted states. It is important for her to do this after she has finished with the drug, otherwise she will not have her full family of states available to her.

First, she could think of how she wants to be when she is talking to her mother and to others. She may want to be different when she talks to her mother and friends than she is when she talks to people at work or acquaintances. So she should think of how she wants to be in talking to different types of people.

It would be good for her to set out at least three empty chairs. Then, she can start by thinking about how she would like to be when she talks to her mother. She can set down in one of the chairs and think about how she wants to communicate with her mother. She can then think about which Resource State is the one Resource State that can best talk to her mother in that way. It may be her Resource State, Kind, or it may be her Resource State, Salesperson. Whichever one it is she can ask this Resource State if it would be willing to help her when she's talking with her mother.

Then, she can stand up and move to the Salesperson chair. As she sets in this chair she can think what it feels like to be in this Salesperson Resource State. It would be good for her to say, 'thank you to this Resource State for being here for me,' to tell this Resource State how important it is for her and how she will continue to want to use it at different times, and also tell it how important her Resource State, Kind, is. It would be good for her to ask Salesperson if it would be willing to continue to help her with the types of conversations that it can best handle. This type of conversation sounds a bit strange, but it is amazing how much difference it can make when the individual states feel appreciated and useful.

While sitting in this, Salesperson, chair it would be good for her to ask Salesperson what she feels about Kind, and have Salesperson to express those feelings directly to Kind in the other chair. The purpose here is for each of the two states, Salesperson, and, Kind, to learn to respect and appreciate each other and learn to compromise and work together.

If one state has difficulty with another state it is good to help educate that state in relation to how useful both states are, and how they are both better off when they can be used for exactly what they are best at.

You may be wondering what the other chair is for, and it may not be needed at all. But, if there is some confusion in terms of which state should be out at particular times Eve could call upon a wise state to help decide. A wise state may be used on the inside sort of like a traffic cop, directing traffic. A wise state may be ask to help decide if it's better to have an angry state out or an assertive state, and in Eve's case a wise state could help decide the times it would be better to have Kind out or to have Salesperson out.

When Eve feels a congruence on the inside, settled on the inside, and feels that her states are getting along and compromising she has done well and this process is finished.

Addictions: Gambling

Why would an intelligent person continue to gamble over and over again, year after year, destroying their financial life and future? Why would someone who understands that casinos make money, lots of money, continued to put money down when it is obvious that over time the casino will take that money away?

These questions seem to have no easy answer. But they do. Compulsive gamblers gamble for a single reason. They are trying to escape. The explanation for this is simple, but first I want to distinguish between compulsive gamblers and recreational gamblers.

Recreational gambling

Recreational gamblers are those people who enjoy gambling, know they will probably lose, but feel the amount that they may lose is worth the joy they get from the experience. They do not gamble to the point that they are risking their financial security. The person who buys a lottery ticket, knowing that the chances are very slim for them to

> **The thing that compels compulsive gamblers to gamble is negative feelings.**

win, but enjoys hearing the reading of the numbers and hoping that their numbers may be chosen is a recreational gambler. Even high rollers who put down millions of dollars are often recreational gamblers if they can easily afford losing the amount they put down. So, it is possible to gamble in a way that does not compromise financial security and in a way that some find enjoyable.

Having a bet with a friend is recreational gambling. "I bet you a 15 minute back rub that my team will win," is recreational gambling. There is nothing wrong with recreational gambling as long as people are not being deceived and financial security is not risked. It can be fun.

Compulsive gambling

Compulsive gambling is another matter. The compulsive gambler is out of control. The compulsive gambler feels compelled to bet. The compulsive gambler suffers from an addictive personality, and may continue to gamble until all ability to gamble is gone, or until financial security is lost. Compulsive gamblers do not have a choice.

The thing that compels compulsive gamblers to gamble is negative feelings. This person is sometimes overwhelmed with bad feelings to the extent that escape is necessary. Casinos have naturally evolved in a way that helps compulsive gamblers escape, because when compulsive gamblers are able to escape by putting their money down casinos make money.

It was probably a plan to build and arrange casinos in a way that best helps compulsive gamblers escape from their anxiety, but it has been found that casinos can make more money by having flashing lights, no clocks, alcoholic drinks, low lights, and a hypnotic environment.

Think about it. A person is overwhelmed by bad feelings. This means they have a Resource State out that is vaded and unresolved. This Resource State feels terrible. The person needs a way to escape the bad feelings. The person needs a way that will put them into another Resource State that is able to zone out and not experienced a bad feeling.

Consider the casino or the one armed bandits. There is the excitement of the possibility of winning money and the threat of losing money. There are flashing lights. There are interesting noises. There are many hypnotic things surrounding the person. In this environment it is easy for the person to zone out and enter into a Resource State that does not have these bad feelings. It is very alluring. Compulsive gambling is an escape from a Vaded Resource State. It makes perfect sense.

There is a reason for everything. If the car does not start there is a reason. It may be out of fuel, there may be something with the wiring that is wrong, or there may be other causes, but there is a reason. If water does not run out of the tap there is a reason. If we get a callous on our foot there is a reason. And, if someone is gambling and is out of control there is a reason. That reason is a Vaded Resource State.

Something has happened in the person's life that has left a Resource State with bad feelings, feeling so bad that the person has a need to escape from those feelings when they come up. The person has a need to escape from the Vaded Resource State when it comes out.

We learned in Chapter 5 that Resource States do not have to remain vaded. Vaded Resource States can become Normal Resource States. This means that compulsive gamblers who are escaping from a Vaded Resource State do not have to continue to escape from the state, because the Vaded Resource State can become Normal and can feel relaxed and supported.

Imagine a traveller who is supposed to stay on the road, who wants to stay on the road, and who intends to stay on the road. A vicious bear runs at the traveller terrifying him so he escapes into the forest. In the forest he feels safe and he can no longer see the bear. This is what it is like for the compulsive gambler. Compulsive gamblers do not want to continue gambling, and they often intend not to gamble but they are forced back into the casino by the vicious bear, the Vaded Resource State. Just as the traveller would not have to escape into the forest if the bear did not scare him the person who has been a compulsive gambler will no longer have a need to escape into the casino if the Resource State that was vaded becomes Normal.

The key to breaking compulsive gambling

The Resource State that is gambling is not the problem. That is a Resource State that is merely helping the person to cope. It is the Vaded Resource State that feels the bad feelings that the gambler is escaping from. It is this state that is still vaded that causes the problem.

It is easy to find a Vaded state that needs healing. All the compulsive gambler needs to do in order to find a Vaded state that needs healing is to attempt to stop gambling. When the compulsive gambler attempts to not gamble the anxiety of the Vaded state will build up. It will not take long.

It is important for the compulsive gambler to be prepared so that when the anxiety builds up, in other words when the Vaded state comes out, the person who has been a compulsive gambler in the past is ready to help heal. All of the techniques that are needed are in Chapter 5 of this book which details how to heal the Vaded state.

A good thing about healing Resource States in this way is that we get benefits even as we heal them. The more we use our techniques for healing Resource States the healthier they become, and as we use the techniques, we begin to feel somewhat better from the start.

Here is what the compulsive gambler needs to do to stop gambling.

- Make up your mind that you no longer want to gamble. Motivation to change helps.
- Read chapter 5 very carefully, learn the steps, and prepare to give the Vaded state the understanding and support it needs when it comes out.
- When you feel compelled to gamble put it off and experience the anxiety of the Vaded state.
- When you know this state is out (and you will), use the steps

> **There will be no compulsion to gamble once the Vaded state is healed.**

you have learned from chapter 5 to bring understanding, support, and healing to the state that has been vaded.
- Any time you feel this Vaded state coming out, continue to use the steps in Chapter 5 until the state that was previously vaded reaches a state of normalcy. At this point you will no longer be out of control.

If good preparation is made prior to feeling the need to gamble it is very likely that the person who has felt unable to keep from gambling in the past will be able to continue to apply the steps from Chapter 5 and never gamble again. Even if a setback happens the motivated person can continue to use the steps until there is no compulsion to gamble.

There will be no compulsion to gamble once the Vaded state is healed. The habit of having gambled will still be present, but that is much easier to deal with than a Resource State that is vaded.

What is meant by 'the habit' is things like friends that were made while gambling that may be missed, or having a place to go for relaxation. Substituting other activities can ensure that nothing is lost and this will help get over the habit much easier.

Those persons who have in the past been compulsive gamblers and who have completed the training and the steps to heal their Vaded state are worthy of praise for the motivation and the work they have completed in order to take control of their lives. It does take a real effort to prepare and be ready to help the Vaded state with nurturance when it comes out. The end result is a Resource State that is comfortable and supported, that is Normal, and a person who is in control of living.

Addictions: Obsessive Compulsive Disorder

Obsessive-compulsive behavior has been mentioned earlier in the book. It is a very interesting disorder. Actually, it is a good coping skill for escaping from the anxiety felt by a Vaded state. It is learned subconsciously and the person with OCD is most often unaware that the high level of focus of the compulsive behavior is a safer place than the bad feelings of the Vaded state.

What causes it

A childhood state has experienced something as a trauma and has had no resolution. These bad feelings occasionally returns when the childhood state comes to the surface. The person learns that by thinking about only a single thing and acting in a single focused way there can be an escape from this childhood state that was out with its bad feelings.

It is much more comfortable to worry about not stepping on cracks than it is to experience the bad feelings held by this childhood state. Since the escape of being zoned out into a compulsive Resource State works so well for the person, the person returns to it over and over again using it more and more, all the time feeling safe while in this obsessive compulsive helper state.

The helper state is really a friend, relieving the negative feelings that would otherwise be felt. But, other Resource States of the person do not see this state as a friend. They see this state that avoids stepping on cracks as a real intrusion in life. They see it as the problem. There is great internal discontent. There are Resource States that often hate each other.

The state that avoids stepping on cracks has a mission of relieving the pain of the bad feelings and fulfilling this mission is of greater importance to it than what the other states think about it.

So, we have a childhood state that has unresolved feelings. This childhood state occasionally comes out experiencing these unresolved feelings. During much of the day this childhood state is not out and the person can carry out their day normally. But, when this childhood state comes out the person has subconsciously learned that by obsessively focusing on some behavior they can escape into a zoned out safe area. It is really quite a simple dynamic. Different individuals will become very creative about what obsession they will focus on.

Many focus on checking locks, others avoid stepping on cracks, some concern themselves with making sure everything is extremely clean or germ-free, and some attempt to do tasks in a different way each time. I knew one woman who feared that she would make a mistake and this would lead to someone else's death. It was almost impossible for her to drive anywhere, because each time she saw a pebble on the road she felt a need to stop and get it off the road so that it could not cause a car accident. She could not put ice in someone's glass because she was afraid the ice might have mixed with it broken glass which could kill the person.

Another individual who lived in a large city obsessed about driving to work on a different route each time. Because it was a large city there were many different combinations of streets that would lead to work, but over a longer period of time this individual had to drive further and further to get to work without going along the same route that had been travelled before.

People with obsessive-compulsive disorder know that their obsession is silly. They wish they could stop, but they have not been able to. This means that many other Resource States understand that the obsession is silly, and they want to stop but they do not understand why it is happening. It would not help them to understand, as the only thing that will help is a resolution of the anxiety felt by the Vaded state.

Psychiatrists have learned that by giving a person who suffers from obsessive-compulsive disorder antidepressants the symptoms sometimes disappear. Often psychiatrists will give a series of different antidepressants hoping to find one that allows the symptoms to disappear. Antidepressants work by blocking states. Different antidepressants block different states. If the psychiatrist finds an antidepressant that is capable of blocking the childhood state feeling the bad feelings then that helper state that goes into the zoned out obsessive-compulsive behavior has no need to come out.

This is no cure, as it leaves the childhood state with the unresolved feelings, but it is a blocking procedure. There are two problems with this,

The person still has the childhood state with unresolved feelings. This cannot be healthy.

Taking a drug is not preferred if there is an alternative. Drugs are expensive, uncomfortable to take and not good for the body.

What needs to change

A much better solution to obsessive-compulsive behavior is to assist the childhood state with the unresolved feelings to feel nurtured, safe, and loved. When this childhood state that carries unresolved feelings can be comfortable and relaxed it will no longer come out experiencing the fears or frustrations of the past. Therefore, the helper state no longer has a need to relieve anxiety by sliding into a zoned out state.

When I first started working with obsessive-compulsive clients I wrongly attempted to work with the Resource State that was carrying out the compulsive behavior. At the time, I saw this Resource State as the problem when it really wasn't. It was just a state trying to help the client feel better. No matter what I did to help convince a state not to come out it would almost always return. This makes sense, because its role was to help the person feel less pain. It would not respond to me, just as it would not respond to other Resource States of the person that did not want it to come out, because when it saw the person in pain it felt compelled to help. It had a job to do.

The solution

First, carefully read the section, "Healing the Vaded state." I say that a lot, don't I? Remember, I said it was the most important part of the book and that it was important to spend time doing the training.

Make sure it is read carefully and the helping hand is charged with a nurturing Resource State. This means that one of your more mature, helping, nurturing states is associated with one of your hands in such a way that when the childhood state comes out feeling upset and compelled to go into obsessive behavior, this hand will be ready to be placed on the part of the body that most feels the anxiety. The message and comfort this helping state brings to the childhood Resource State gives the Vaded state an opportunity to feel supported, empowered, and resolved.

The most important aspect of healing the state that is causing obsessive-compulsive behavior is to make sure the right state is out during the healing process. This is not difficult to do. The anxiety state comes out immediately before the excessive compulsive behavior begins.

> **When you feel compelled to begin the obsessive-compulsive behavior that growing feeling of being compelled is the Vaded state coming out.**

A good way to make sure that the Vaded state is out so that it can get the release it needs and deserves is to avoid doing obsessive-compulsive behavior.

It will not take long. When you feel compelled to begin the obsessive-compulsive behavior that growing feeling of being compelled is the Vaded state coming out. The childhood state that has unresolved feelings is coming out. The longer you keep from doing the excessive compulsive behaviour the more anxiety you will feel.

When you are feeling anxious remember your helping hand that has been charged by one of your nurturing Resource States. Realize what part of the body that is feeling the most anxious. It might be your head. It might be your chest. It might be your stomach. It might be over a large area, or over a small area. This is where you are feeling the Vaded state. Bring your helping hand to this part of your body and remember the messages of your helping state, this thing you fear is in the past, it isn't really here now so you can shrink it to any size, you can clear it away from your inner space completely, and you can receive a hug and loving support from the helping hand pressing down.

You can move your helping hand to different parts of your body that may feel the need of support, love, and empowerment. Make sure you press the thumb down giving a loving hug that carries the message, "I will be with you always."

Do not feel bad about the anxiety; feel supportive of the part that feels it. This child part of you that had been vaded by negative experience in the past can learn to feel accepted and powerful and loved. A good thing about using your helping state, your helping hand, is that the more it is used with positive intent, the stronger it becomes. The more you use it the better it works. Just make sure you always maintain the positive intent to help the upset states. It will feel good to this helping part to be appreciated and respected by the other Resource States. It is always best for the Resource States to respect and honor each other so that they can feel good about themselves.

Addictions: Compulsive spending

Shopping is good. Compulsive shopping is not.

Mary feels uneasy. There is a general anxiety that compels her to shop. Through experience, she knows that if she goes shopping the anxiety that she is feeling will subside. She feels pushed to shop almost like a drug addict is pushed to take a drug. She may buy things that she does not need. Something about shopping, looking at pretty things, trying things on, and purchasing are an escape for her. Mary suffers from compulsive spending.

Compulsive spending is an addiction. It is an escape from negative feelings, an escape from feelings of anxiety, into an activity where release can be found. Compulsive shopping is a coping skill where a person feels out of control while using it. It can be expensive, and the person may find that they are spending more than they can afford. Even if the person can afford the amount that is being spent in their compulsive shopping, it is not good to live out of control.

There is nothing wrong with shopping.

Compulsive spending is treated in the same way that any

addiction is treated. What is important is that the state that feels anxious, the state that compels the person to shop, receives a resolution so that the person is no longer out of control.

There is nothing wrong with shopping. We have to shop to buy what we need, and it can be fun. There's nothing wrong with shopping to have fun as long as we feel in control, as long as we do not feel compelled to shop.

Some compulsive shoppers buy clothes that they will never wear. They may have collections of things bigger than they would ever use in a lifetime. They may be constantly out of money because of their compulsion to shop.

When the Vaded Resource State that compels the person to shop receives the resolution it needs it will no longer come to the surface with anxiety so the person who was a compulsive shopper will be able to decide to shop and buy as they choose.

The Resource State to focus on for compulsive shopping is the Resource State that feels anxiety, the Resource State that compels a person to shop. This is the Resource State that comes out feeling uneasy and anxious immediately before the decision to go shopping. It is most likely a child Resource State feeling fearful or holding feelings of rejection and loneliness.

The techniques presented in Chapter 5 to resolve the Vaded Resource State will be helpful to the compulsive shopper, following the careful training presented there. **This process will only work when both a nurturing state has been found and trained, and when the anxious state is currently out, feeling**

anxiety. It is easy to make sure the anxious state is out. It will come out with feelings of anxiety pushing you to shop.

When you feel upset and compelled to shop do these 3 steps to resolve your Vaded state:

1. Remember the helping hand is there for you. This is your helping Resource State.
2. At the time you feel compelled to shop notice the part of your body that feels the most anxiety and press your helping hand there and share unconditional love.
3. Think about nurturing the part that feels uneasy and share loving acceptance with it. Prove this part that it is lovable.

After using these steps and after the anxiety subsides it is good to ask oneself, "Now that I am in control, what do I really want to do with my time?"

When the previously vaded state feels free from the past, feels supported and safe, the person will be able to make decisions about what is really wanted. It would be OK if that decision was to shop, as long as it was a freely made decision, not one made from a sense of being out of control. Obviously, the decision may be something entirely different. People will often make the comment, "It's OK now. I have a choice."

It is good, as adults, to have things that we really want to do. Too often people will fill their lives with what they should do, or with what they feel compelled to do. Sure, there are things we need to do to carry out our responsibilities, but there are also opportunities to do what we want. Often children are good at knowing what they want. It is good, as adults, to feel free to consider what we want, as a child would. What really makes us happy when we are free to choose?

Chapter 12: Depression

From inside depression it is difficult to see outside. When one is depressed it seems like the whole life has been depressed. Depression can be caused by an organic, physiological problem or it can be caused by a psychological issue. Most depressions are caused by psychological issues, and that is what this chapter will be about.

Psychological depression is the result of perceived reality not matching expectations. It does not matter as much what the life situation is, as much as whether the life situation matches what is expected. I once taught at a university where there had been several government cutbacks on expenditure. The people who had taught there for several years were quite distressed about the jobs they had to do. They had to work longer hours, coordinate more things, and have less time to teach the same things that they had been teaching. Their conversations reflected an upset mood about their workload.

At the same time new staff were being added. These new staff who had not been exposed to previous conditions in the workplace thought they had landed a wonderful job. The number of hours they had to work per week seemed less than they were working at their old jobs, and they were very pleased at the conditions.

In this example the staff that had been at the university for several years were dealing with the exact same conditions that the new staff were but their expectations were very different. The long-term staff were distressed and upset at their conditions and the new staff were pleased with exactly the same conditions.

The same thing happens with depression. A person who expected life to be different than it is may be depressed about their situation. Depression is not a decision, but it is a reaction to the realization that life is not what was expected. This disjunct between what is and what is expected can be brought about by many different things. Obviously, the loss of a loved one who we expected would live longer can bring about depression, as can the loss of a relationship that we expected would last longer.

Sometimes we can become depressed over things that we knew would happen, but we still had not aligned expectations to match what we knew would happen. For example, aging can bring about depression. Looking in the mirror and seeing an older face look back and feeling the effects of aging can bring about depression.

Aging is much less likely to bring about depression if the person has been more fully aware of the aging process and thought more positively about people going through the process.

Those people who are critical of older people are more likely to be depressed when they become older. Those people who are critical about handicapped people are more likely to become depressed if they become handicapped.

The person who sees someone who is blind as a full person leading a full life relying more on highly sensitized senses of sound and smell will be less likely to become depressed if they themselves become blind.

Some people become depressed over the loss of a pet, over failing at school, loss of physical ability, over the loss of virginity, over contracting a disease, over noticing a change in how they look, over loneliness, over an awareness that they are not who they thought they were toward others, and over a multitude of other things. All of these things have in common that what is preferred to be reality is not reality.

An interesting thing about depression in terms of Resource States is that while the whole body feels depressed not all Resource States are depressed. Often only a single Resource State is depressed. This Resource State feels so bad about its situation it doesn't give permission to any other Resource State to have a good time. It is similar to the man or woman who discovers that their partner is having an affair. One Resource State can be so upset about the affair that it refuses to allow any other Resource State to enjoy the relationship. The Resource State that enjoys conversation at breakfast is not allowed to do that, the Resource State that enjoys sex is not allowed to do that, a Resource State that feels positive about the partner is not allowed to do that.

When one Resource State is depressed it can be like a semi-trailer turned sideways on the freeway blocking all lanes of traffic. It is not going to let anything else through. It has decided that life is bad and it does not give permission for any other state to enjoy it.

Antidepressants

It is best if depression can be alleviated without drugs. Drugs work by blocking Resource States. Antidepressant drugs block Resource States from coming to the executive and feeling as much as they normally would. Therefore, someone on antidepressants may report feeling as if they are living life from under a blanket. If possible, it is better to have our Resource States clear and free. That does not mean that antidepressants should never be used and that decision is between you and your doctor or psychiatrist. Antidepressants are sometimes the best course of action.

The Resource State that is depressed needs respect and understanding. It is better for it to hear that it is understandable that it is be upset rather than to hear that it is silly that it is upset. It needs to become cooperative so it will allow other Resource States to have energy and enjoy aspects of living even before it can realign its expectations with reality.

A well-trained Resource State therapist will find and get permission from the depressed state for a couple of other Resource States to enjoy things that they have always enjoyed, like going to the library, taking a walk, or surfing the Internet. When the depressed state is empathized with and gives permission for some Resource States to enjoy living the individual will immediately begin to feel somewhat better.

It is still important for the depressed state to find a way it can contribute in the world as it is. For example, if a woman who was pleased with her appearance was in a fire and her face was burned the Resource State that applied makeup, and helped to make the face beautiful might become depressed. This Resource State might have felt very important and felt that it was very important for the woman to be beautiful.

The first step that a skilled therapist would use in working with this Resource State would be to show understanding that this state is upset, and indicate that being upset is a normal reaction. The therapist would then find exactly what the role of the depressed Resource State was. Its role might be to create beauty and to be pleased with this creation, to create something the woman could be proud of. The Resource State might be named Artist, or Beauty Creator. This Resource State might be encouraged to do some type of artwork which it could be proud of. The therapist would convey to the depressed Resource State that its new role is in no way parallel to its old role, but that it is something that is important, in that it is a way it can contribute. The depressed Resource State can be encouraged to allow other Resource States to enjoy their time and it can be congratulated on the way it has learned to help by being an artist, and contribute.

When someone becomes depressed it is unlikely that their old expectation will ever be met, therefore the Resource State that has become depressed needs to set a new expectation that can be met. Depression often comes with grief and sadness. Depression can be thought of as complicated bereavement. Rather than experiencing the sadness of the loss and moving on to another role the depressed Resource State carries the illusion that because the expectation can never be met life can never be good.

It is okay for a state to grieve and to be sad, and these are natural aspects of healing. Over time, the pain of grief and sadness diminishes. What is important is that the grieving Resource State finds a positive role for itself and for that state to give permission to other states to enjoy living. A Resource State needs to be happy with its role, and it needs to take on a role that it is interested in and has the skills to do.

Chapter 13: Anger

Anger is a normal human emotion. We all experience anger and this starts at a very young age, as any parent knows. Recognizing and expressing our anger is very healthy. A few years ago in 1991 a British researcher, Eysenck, reported a series of studies relating to our ability to recognize and express our emotions. He, and others, found that our ability to do this is highly related to our health. He gave a test that divided people into four groups on their ability to recognize and express their emotions, and he found that those who could recognize and express their emotions the best (type 4) had 10 times less cancer than those who could recognize and express their emotions least best (type 1).

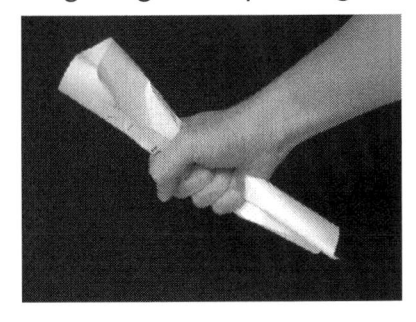

He took a group of 100 people who were in the two least best groups (type 1 and type 2) at recognizing and expressing their emotions and randomly divided them into two groups of 50 to ensure that the two groups were as equal to each other as possible.

One of the two equal groups was given counseling for the purpose of learning to recognize and express their emotions. The other group acted as a control group and received no counseling. Thirteen years later a follow-up data collection revealed that in the group that had received no counseling 16 people had died of cancer. In the group that had received counseling not one had died of cancer.

This is an amazing finding. It points to the fact that how we deal with our emotions has the big impact, not only with how we feel but on our health, as well. It is most likely that even individuals who have the best mental health will occasionally die from cancer, but studies like this one reveal that they will less often.

Eyensak (1991) also reported more specifically about anger and its relationship to coronary heart disease. When 92 people from the group that was least effective/skilled at expressing their anger were randomly divided into two groups of 46 the group that had counseling to improve their recognition of anger and expression of anger had better health. After the 13 years only 3 people in the group that had counseling had died of coronary related diseases while 16 people in the group who did not have counseling had died of coronary related diseases.

These studies indicate how important it is for us to be able to recognize and express our emotions appropriately for our health. It is also important for us to be able to do this in terms of the peace that we feel on the inside. If we carry with us anger that is repressed and unresolved it is a heaviness on the inside. We do not have internal peace. We put a stress on our systems that can result in disease.

We need to express our feelings, but we need to learn how to express them in a way we can feel good about later. If we express anger in a way that we do not feel comfortable it can be embarrassing and it can make us feel not as positive about ourselves. We can feel out of control. We can damage some relationships and lose others.

These are a few things that we need to learn about anger.

- We all get angry.
- It is unhealthy to hang onto anger and not express it.
- It is not good to express anger in a way that we do not feel good about later.
- It is a gift to others to let them know in an appropriate way how we honestly feel.

Here are some myths about anger.

- I used to get angry but I don't anymore.
- I cannot control my anger.
- What I do is not my fault. Other people make me do it.

We all get angry

Some people hold the illusion that they no longer get angry. A person may say, "I used to get angry but I have not been angry in years." This is a person who is out of touch with feelings. If we are alive we feel love, sadness, excitement, anger, and other feelings. A problem is that the surface state may not be the one that is feeling these things; therefore we may be unconscious to them.

This is not living. If we are not feeling while we are here we are more like a robot than a human.

It is not our thoughts that define who we are. It is our feelings. If we are out of touch with our feelings and we are not recognizing them this is not good for ourselves or for those around us.

It is very frustrating to be around a person that shows no feelings. This sense is, "I can't get through to him." There is a lot of reality to that sense. It is pretty accurate. The frustration of not hearing what someone feels from that person feels like an incompleteness, and it is. It is a gift to those around us to be honest and open about our feelings, to share with them the truth about what is going on inside us, but this is hard to do if we do not know what is going on inside.

Emotional intelligence is our ability to recognize our feelings and to express them. There are many of us who are not high on emotional intelligence. This is not healthy, it is not living, and it is frustrating to those around us.

Sometimes loved ones will get so frustrated that they literally want to shake a person to get their feelings out. Often they know them well enough to know what they feel, but the person will not admit to feelings or discuss them. This person probably does not know his or her own feelings.

So how do we learn to recognize when we are angry? When a person feels angry it is not all of the Resource States of the person that feel angry. The Resource State that feels angry may be underlying and not at the surface. A first step in learning to recognize when we feel angry is to be aware of the situation that would likely make us angry.

For example, if someone destroys something that is precious to us and shows no concern about what they have done, stop and give yourself some time to explore what the different parts of you feel. A surface intellectual part may rationalize that it was just an object and that it was of little consequence. But there may be an underlying part that feels hurt and angry about the disregard the person has shown to you.

There may be times when our own actions signify that we are angry when we had not recognized it before. You may find yourself having a short fuse with others for no apparent reason. This can be an indication that one of your Resource States is angry about something.

We may find ourselves feeling upset about how other people drive, about politics, or about life in general. A cranky person is often an angry person who is not expressing feelings appropriately.

A big first step in allowing an angry Resource State an opportunity to express what it feels is to give it permission to feel angry. Some people disrespect anger and think of it as a weakness. Anger is no weakness. It is more of a weakness to deny that it exists than to recognize and express it.

A Resource State that is angry needs to feel like it has permission to come to the surface and express itself. It needs to feel it has permission to be little and weak and upset. It needs to be congratulated for its willingness to say what it feels. Feelings need to flow through rather than to stagnate. An angry Resource State needs to be celebrated, needs to be appreciated, and needs to be heard.

When these things happen we will become much more able to quickly recognize and express our anger. If the anger we feel does not seem to be appropriate for what we have experienced, it may be that a Vaded Resource State is coming out with anger that it holds about something else that happened earlier on in life. If this is the case the steps in the chapter on healing the Vaded Resource State will help this Resource State resolve the earlier unresolved feelings that it holds.

In order to better feel our anger we can remember a time when we were angry in the past. Think about something that really made you angry. It may be something a few years ago or even in childhood. Think about where you were, what was done, and what you felt being right there. Think about how big you are there and about what it was like for you right at that time.

This brings this Resource State out that has been able to be angry in the past and when you get it out, ask it what you can call it. What is a good name for it? You need to get this name from the Resource State. Then when you get the name of this state that is able to feel anger, call it by its name, thank it for being one of your resources, and ask it if it would be willing to help you experience the upset times that you have today.

By doing this you are asking an underlying Resource State that has the ability to feel anger to help you today. This Resource State does not have to be the one that expresses the anger to others, but it can be very useful in allowing you to feel anger and recognize that it is there.

It is good to give praise to this Resource State for the important role that it will help you with. It is also good to let this Resource State know that it will be helped to release this anger appropriately, to let it flow through.

An open and free life is one where feelings are felt completely and are allowed to flow through the body and mind, they are accepted and appreciated, and have an opportunity to be released.

This is the first part of dealing with anger, recognizing it, and feeling it. The next part is learning how to express it to others.

Expressing anger appropriately

I have already mentioned that unrecognized anger can cause a person to be cranky and feel upset by the little things that other people do. Unrecognized anger can result in a passive aggressive behavior. The person will not admit they are upset but they take it out on the other person anyway. There's real dishonesty in this, often to both the person who feels the anger and also to the person who winds up being the punching bag.

So, one type of inappropriate expression of anger is passive aggressive behavior. The person says there is nothing wrong, but their actions reveal there is something wrong. This can be conscious or unconscious. The person dishing out the passive-aggressive behavior may be aware of what they are doing and why, or they may be totally unaware of why they are doing it.

Let's say a couple has a fifth wedding anniversary coming up on Friday. They had discussed earlier that they would go out and have a celebratory dinner and one partner is looking forward to this dinner with much anticipation. They each feel positive about the relationship, about their partner, and about the good time they will have on Friday night. The other partner forgets about Friday night and schedules something else during that timeslot.

A non-passive aggressive way to handle this would be to be straightforward about feelings. If the partner who was really looking forward to the Friday night dinner can recognize their feelings that partner may tell how much they were looking forward to it, how much they appreciated the relationship, how upset they felt and how let down they felt by their partner not sharing their excitement.

A passive aggressive way of responding to the situation would be to say, "It's no big deal," and then go about giving the cold shoulder to the other partner and withholding love and support. Some people might go so far as to 'accidentally' destroy items that belong to their partner.

There is nothing wrong with saying to someone, "I want to be honest with you. I feel really upset about what has happened. You are important to me, but there is part of me that is angry with you right now. I don't want to feel that way, but part of me does." This is honest.

Out of control anger

Some people talk about being out of control when they are angry. They say that when they get in a rage state they cannot control themselves. This can be possible. A Resource State can have as a role, rage. It may be that this Resource State has as part of this role not to listen to other Resource States or other people while it is out. This can be dangerous both for the person who has a state like this, and for others who this person may come in contact with when this rageful state emerges.

There are a few things that can help us understand how this person can gain control of their actions. One of the things is that the rageful state does not think much. That is not its role. It cannot maintain rage and consider things in a thoughtful way at the same time. Because of this it cannot make a decision about when it comes out. It is a bit like having a big powerful vicious dog that will respond when told to attack but otherwise it does not interfere. Therefore, for a rage state to come out it has to be called out, and given permission to come out by other states.

The rage state is there to help. It wants to help and like any other state it does not like not being liked.

What happens with a lot of people who go into rage is that afterward they feel bad about it. They may really regret some of the things they said or things they did. They may say things like, "I hate myself when I'm like that." They may even wish they never got like that.

All of these messages can be heard by this rage state that is there to help. The rage state can hear the criticism and has probably heard it so long that it has given up on the chance it could ever be accepted and liked by the other states. But, it would still like to be liked, even if it might not admit it. This is useful information in helping a rage state to find a role that is beneficial to the person, a role that the other states can appreciate.

Another interesting thing is that there are only certain times this rage state will come out. It might come out in a bar or at home, but it might not come out in the office. It might not come out in front of a loved grandmother. It does not come out at random. It comes out when it is called out by another state.

This being called out is in the control of the person, even though the rage state may not be. There is always a decision to call the state out, or not. There is power in this. If a person who has a rage state really wants to have control of their anger they can. They can have control by working with the states that call out the rage state. If you have a rage state that comes out causing you to feel out of control here is what you can do.

If you have a rage state here is what you can do.

Sit down in a comfortable chair, relax, and think about a time when you experienced this rage state. Think about what was happening before you went into rage. Imagine the scene exactly, what was said, what you felt, and what you thought. There will be a moment when there is permission given to be angry and out of control. It may sound something like one of these, "They cannot do that to me. I will not stand for it. That's too much for me to handle."

After hearing these internal messages you will probably remember feeling a surge of adrenaline or energy and a sense of going out of control. It is those messages that you hear and how they are heard that are calling the rage state to come out. It may be that the wrong state has a job of deciding how you should handle anger.

Remember, anger is a natural feeling and there is nothing wrong with feeling angry. And remember, your rage state is your friend. It is there to help you. It is not helping you by being out at the wrong time, but it could help you if it were to come out at the right time.

If you were to be threatened by a pack of wild dogs, or a group of hoodlums down a dark alleyway and your life is in danger it would be wonderful to have a rage state to come out with a lot of power and energy to defend you. You can be thankful that you have this state that could help you if your life was ever threatened, but this is the wrong state to have out talking to a friend or an acquaintance. Let's find a better state to bring out.

Finding an Assertive Resource State

It is good to have an assertive state that can express anger or feelings of being upset in a way that allows you to feel that you said what needed to be said in an appropriate way. Think about a time when you have, in the past, been assertive. When have you told anyone, "I'm sorry, but I don't like the way you're doing that?" When have you ever been firm in expressing yourself to someone else, firm but respectful? It may be a time when you were young. It may be a time at work or with a family member. It could be any time.

If you can think of the time that you have been firm and respectful go to the time now in your head. Think about exactly where you were, what you said, and how you felt. Imagine being there right now and imagine feeling the way you did while you were being assertive. Now, get a name for this part of yourself. While feeling this assertive state, ask yourself, "What would be a good name for this part of me?"

Once you get a name for this part of yourself address it directly calling it by name and ask it if it would be willing to help you when you want to express what you're feeling to someone in a firm but in an assertive way. Parts love to have more time out, and they love to be more useful, therefore it is most likely that this part will be happy to help you if it is called out to help when you are feeling angry and when you want to express yourself without the rage state.

If you have been able to locate an assertive part of yourself and you have been able to do this then you are ready for the next step a bit further below.

If you have not located an assertive state

Some people are not able to locate an assertive state that they have used. You may be one of those people and if you are it's okay. It is not a problem. You will still have a state that can take on an assertive role.

Think of someone who is assertive at times in the way that you would like to be. It may be a friend, it may be an actor, or it may be a made-up person in your own mind. Ask yourself, "How would this person handle situations like I am confronted with?" What would they do, and what would they say? How would they present themselves and how would they feel while expressing themselves?

While you are thinking about these things you are in a Resource State that has a good handle on what it is like to be assertive. While you are thinking about these things you are in a good Resource State that can help you be assertive. Ask this Resource State that understands assertiveness, what would be a good name for it. Ask this part of yourself, "What can I call this part of myself?"

When you get a name for this part of yourself you can call it by name and ask it, "Since you have such a good handle on assertiveness, would you be willing to be the assertive part of me and respond when I need your skills? Again, Resource States love to have bigger roles, and they love to be out. It is most likely that this state will be happy to help you, happy to respond in the way that it knows and understands when it is called out.

Now that you have a Resource State that can respond assertively

Now that you have a Resource State that can respond assertively all you need to do is to make sure that this is the Resource State that is called out when it is needed, and that the rage state, will be there to protect you if your life is in danger. In order to control this you will need to locate the state that makes a decision on how to respond to anger.

Again, think of the time when you responded inappropriately when you were angry. Think of the point of decision when you decided this was a time to really be angry, a time to call up the rage state. What do you feel like right now thinking how to respond to this difficult situation? This is another way of asking, "What does this part of you that has called out the rage state feel like?" It may feel weak or feel like it does not want to be taken advantage of, or even abused. Get a name for this part of yourself in the same way that you have done before. Ask it, feeling as it does, what would be a good name for this part. Getting names for parts is extremely important in order to make lasting changes.

Call it by name and ask it if it would be willing to use the assertive state rather than the rage state during all the times that the body is not in a life-threatening situation. See how you feel when you ask this decision-making state this question. Does it feel like this state is the correct state to make this decision? If you have a sense that this state cannot make a good decision you can ask it if it's okay for another state to make this decision at times when you are angry. If this state does feel it can make the decision to call the assertive state out that is fine, it can be used. But if it does not feel it is the best state to make the decision to call the assertive state out you can use a wiser part of yourself to make those decisions at those times.

If you need to find a wiser part of yourself to help you at these decision times then quietly ask yourself for a part that could best decide which state would be good to respond to anger. This can be sort of like a traffic cop on the inside directing the right Resource State to come out. You will be able to feel a part that has the ability to decide when to call out the assertive state or to call out the rage state if your life is in danger. Get a name for this 'traffic cop' state on the inside. It could be "Wise" or any other name. Ask it if it would be willing to make the best decision about how to express anger by calling the best state out.

Now, you have an assertive state that is happy to help and you have a state that is happy to call on the assertive state when you feel angry, or to call on your rage state if your life is threatened. You need to show some appreciation to the rage state and let it know that it can now be internally respected by all states. They can all be glad that it is there protecting them. It will feel good to your rage state to know that it is internally respected and appreciated, and this will help it feel good about its new role of coming out only when the body is physically threatened.

Focus on all of these states, the **assertive part of you**, **the part of you that decides which state to come out**, and **the rage part of you**, and have an internal handshake so they can each be happy with their roles and each be happy with the roles of the other states. You can think of them all being on the same team, with the same colored jumpers.

I will now provide a summary of the steps to gain control of anger, and to express it appropriately. **These steps are provided only as a summary** for what you have already read and they are not provided to act as steps that provide enough information about what to do without reading this chapter on anger, and other chapters in the book that it refers to.

Steps to control anger
1. Sit down, relax, and think about the time right before you have gone into rage in the past.
2. Get a name for the part of you that has in the past called out the rage state.

3. Find a time you have been assertive in the past or think of the qualities of someone who is assertive to locate a part of yourself that can act as your assertive state.
4. Get a name for this part of you that can act as your assertive state and ask it if it will be willing to help you express your anger appropriately in the future.
5. Return to the state that has made the decision in the past about how anger will be handled and see if this state is able to ask the assertive state to come out to express feelings at times when the body is angry but is not physically threatened.
6. If this state is not the best state to call out your assertive state find a wise state that can make the decision to call out the assertive state to express feelings.
7. Encourage all states to respect each other and appreciate that each has a role to do on the inside.
8. Think of a time when in the past you would have been rageful and use imagery to practise using the assertive part now.

There are different ways you can express your anger appropriately now that you have the tools. There may be times when you are not able to say the things that you would really like to say because it would be stupid to do so. For example, if you have a job that you like and that you would like to keep it might not be appropriate to express anger to a boss who has his own psychological issues.

Some people are very poor at hearing the feelings of others and this is something that needs to be taken into consideration. It is good to be wise in terms of what can be said and how it can be said. It may be there are some people that you cannot express anger to at all without them having a reaction that you do not want to deal with. If this is the case it is still important for you to be able to express your feelings, and you can do this with friends or family. You can tell them how your boss made you feel, and how difficult it was for you to deal with a person who is incapable of hearing what you would really like to say in a respectful and assertive way.

Whenever possible, it is appropriate to tell people how you feel. It is also respectful. If someone is upset with you about the way you are doing something it is your right to know their feelings. Otherwise you might keep doing something that you would not like to do just because they did not tell you how they really feel. They would be showing respect to you to tell you in a nice way what they are feeling.

In the same way you are showing respect to others if you tell them your true feelings. This needs to be done wisely. There's no need to hurt someone just to be honest about feelings or thoughts. If you think someone looks fat, that doesn't necessarily mean you should tell them. But, if you think they are taking advantage of you, then whenever possible, it is appropriate to help them.

You can think of it as being loving. The golden rule states that you should do onto others as you would have them do unto you. Being honest with your feelings is the same thing. Think about how you would like it if it were reversed. Then, using your assertive state say how you're really feeling in a diplomatic way.

Here's an example. "I care a lot about you and always will, but part of me is very upset."

You will have to use your intuition and intelligence to know what the right thing to say is and how it should be said. It is loving and respectful for friends to be upfront and honest with each other about the things that they have a right to know. It is an art to tell them well.

Chapter 14: Grieving

Births and deaths are amazing moments in life. There is something about being near the beginning or the end of life that brings us closer to meaning. Births are normally experienced as times for celebration. When someone we love dies there is often a deep sadness.

Grieving can be a bittersweet experience. Along with the sorrow of loss is a celebration of the relationship. It is the appreciation of the relationship that goes hand-in-hand with the sad feeling of having lost it. Tears of loss and happiness of having had the relationship can be intertwined.

There are some aspects of grieving that are natural and healing. There are also experiences some people have during their grieving process that are complicated by bereavement. The loss can be the straw that broke the camel's back because there were issues that were already present.

It is natural to feel deep sadness, to feel loss, to feel a yearning that the other person is still here. It is normal to cry without being able to control when. Some people cry without tears. It is normal in the early stages of grieving to feel overwhelmed, and to question, "How am I going to get through this?" During the first few days it is normal to feel angry, sometimes at another person, sometimes at the person who died, sometimes at ourselves, and sometimes at God.

Sadness is not a heavy emotion. It can be deep and overwhelming, but within sadness is love. The sadness after the loss of a loved one will never completely go away but it does subside. Time allows us to look back with layers of later experiences between the loss and today.

When we experience those normal aspects of grieving it is our job to continue living as best we can. It is positive while doing this to realize the gift that we had during the time that we had the relationship. This is paying respect to the relationship while at the same time it helps us deal with the grieving process. It is good to know that grieving may take months or years, and that we have no responsibility to make it take longer than it does. It does not honor the loved one to grieve any more or any longer than the process takes. There will be a time when flowers will smell good again and the beautiful sunsets will be noticed.

Complicated Grieving

There are things that people sometimes experience that complicate the grieving process. These things keep us from moving on through the grieving process in a natural and normal way. After the first few days holding on to anger, blame, guilt, or a deep sense of having not said something are feelings that slow and inhibit the grieving process. If, after the first few days, it is clear that you are experiencing one of these heavy emotions then something needs to be done to help you get back onto a path of loving grieving.

We want positive feelings around the lost loved one, and we want the impression we hold of them to be that of a beautiful garden full of only beautiful things. In order to have this we need to let go of any dark emotion such as anger, blame, guilt, or a deep sense of not having said something.

In order to move away from complicated grieving we need to know about introjects. An introject is our internalized impression of another person. Each of our Resource States have their own introjects, internalized impressions of others. One of our Resource States may have an impression of 'mother' as nurturing and loving while another Resource State may have an impression of her as being controlling or harsh. This is totally normal.

Child Resource States may feel disempowered by bigger adult introjects that they hold onto in the inside. In a similar way if we are feeling anger, blame, guilt, or a deep sense of having not said something, we have a Resource State that is being impacted by introjects, by our internalized impressions of another person or persons. Having this knowledge gives us the power to get back to a loving grieving process.

Here is what you can do if after the first few days of grieving you are holding some of these heavy and negative emotions. Do this only when you feel ready, but when you feel ready it can be an experience that will get you back onto a loving grieving process.

Put two chairs facing each other about the distance apart where two people could sit and talk. Sit down in one of the chairs and look at the empty chair you are facing. Think about, if your lost loved one were sitting in that chair now, what you would like him or her to know. Think about those things that you did not get a chance to say or that you did not say that you would like them to know. Think about your feelings toward the person, love, blame, anger, respect, or any other feelings. Some people have feelings of concern about how their loved one died.

Now, invite the essence of your loved one into that chair. When you feel their essence in the chair say out loud, directly to their essence all those things you feel like saying to him or her. You can speak honestly of love, blame, anger, and respect, whatever you feel. Tell them how it has been without them and anything else you want to say.

When you have finished saying absolutely everything you would like to say, stand up and move over to the chair of your loved one. Now, as you sit in the chair of your loved one, experience being this introject, this person, and respond back as if your loved one were speaking to you. Say whatever feels like comes from their higher, loving self to you.

When you have finished allowing your loved one to speak (to you) to your chair, stand up and move back to your own chair and set down. Finish the process by saying anything else you feel like saying to your loved one. It is important that you feel completely expressed in an honest and loving way.

You can do the same process inviting the introjects of other people into the empty chair to help deal with your feelings of anger, blame, or guilt that you might have in relation to them. For example, if your loved one was killed in a car crash involving a drunken driver you could ask the introject of the person who had been drunk into the empty chair and say everything you would like to say to this person. Then, you can move to the chair of the person you've spoken to, feel what they feel, and allow them to respond to you. To do this you can think of yourself as a great actor really going into the skin of the other person, forgetting yourself, and just honestly saying what the other person feels and wants to say. Again, speak out load it whatever feels that their higher, loving self wants to say to you.

If you are angry at God you can ask the essence of God into the empty chair and say everything that you want to say to God. Obviously, if you imagine God to be everywhere then that includes the empty chair. After saying everything that you would like to say move over and sit in God's chair. Respond to yourself honestly feeling your sense of what God wants to say. Then move back to your chair and respond one more time to God.

Whoever you feel anger toward, whoever you blame, whoever you feel guilty about in relation to your grief you can use this process. Be honest and sincere in what you say while sitting in both chairs. This process allows feelings to be expressed and it allows a sense of understanding.

This same process also works with the loss of a pet. You can invite the essence of your pet into the empty chair and speak directly to it the things that you would like to say, and when you set in your pet's chair you can allow it to have the language to speak back to you.

You can likewise give voice to a lost fetus or baby in the same way, making sure the child is given its higher loving voice to speak to you.

Remember, the best way to honor your lost loved one is to be able to surround the memory with positivity, without holding onto the heavy, negative emotions, so that the memory is a positive one. We want our lives to be blessed by the love we have been able to experience.

This is true also for the other things we grieve. In order to grieve we had to have something worth grieving. Whether it is the loss of a relationship due to breakup, the loss of youth, beauty, health, or anything else, part of the grieving process should be to have a sense of thanks for having been able to live for a time with something or someone who is worth grieving about. We can also be thankful that we have allowed ourselves enough openness to have a connection strong enough to grieve.

The most living part of life is connectedness.

Spring

The shining sun and whispering hum that flirts with grass and tree,

Announce with easy calm and subtle strength, tranquilly to me,

That winter's gone and life goes on and birds can fill the air,

And healing is what nature does while I was standing there.

Chapter 15: Self esteem

What is your name? What do you think and feel about who you are? If I really got to know you do you think I would see you as a good person? Would I like you? Are you a good person? How good are you at doing things, different things? Would you be a good friend?

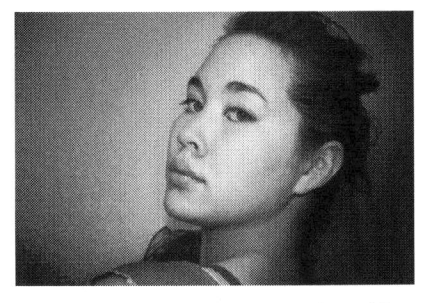

What we think and feel about ourselves is very important. We all know people who seem to have a high self-concept even though they may not be very talented or accomplished, and we also know people who are extremely talented and accomplished with a low self-concept.

There seems to be little relationship between how good someone is at something and their self-concept, or between their self-concept and how good a friend they might be. Self-concept must then be based on something other than ability, something other than friendship. It is.

Some people live their lives struggling trying to be good enough. It seems like no matter what they do they always struggle in an attempt to please others. And it seems like no matter what they do they are never quite able to feel like they have done that.

The constant struggle keeps them from being able to relax, to be in the moment, to decide what they want to do as opposed to what might please others. They are robbing themselves of their own life experience, and they are robbing others from being able to know who they really are. It is a waste.

This life is so amazing, just to be able to live and breathe, touch and feel, to relate and interrelate. It is a sad waste to go through it focused on someone else's wishes, on what someone else thinks, rather than just being honest and just living in the moment.

It is good to respect others and take their wishes into consideration, but we need to be true to ourselves, and true to others by being who we really are. That is the kindest and most respectful thing we can do. We want our friends to be honest with us and it is good to be honest with them too.

Every person is a good person if they allow themselves to be who they really are. Bad things are done as an emotional reaction because we don't feel good enough. When we feel just as good as anyone and we feel comfortable in our own skin then we do not have a need to take, hurt, or react in a negative way. We don't have a need to put someone else down.

When we are happy with ourselves we have an ability to allow other people to be themselves. Getting to know people is one of the most wonderful things. It is not wonderful to be around someone who is pretending to be something they are not just so they will be liked or accepted. That is actually a bit boring. A person who is real and honest is not boring. We are only boring when we are pretending to be something that we are not.

I hear some people saying, "But I can't keep from pretending." I think it is more accurate to say, "I don't know how to keep from pretending," or even, "I don't think I can keep from pretending." I like these statements better. They are more accurate, because the truth is that the change can be made to be yourself if that is what you want.

You can continue to live a life that is not your own, to live a life in fear of someone knowing who you are, or you can make another choice. I'm sure you know people who present their real selves. Those people say what they feel like saying, usually in a respectful and diplomatic way, often in a loving way. They are self-confident and self-accepting, and they usually accept others. You can be that way too.

Where does the fear come from?

What is it that causes you to fear being not good enough? The answer is easy and it is the same answer that is repeated many times in this book. It is a Vaded state. If you feel that you cannot please others it is because, as a child there was a time when you felt a deeply upset because you felt you could not please someone who is important to you. You may have felt unlovable.

The Resource State you were in at the time became vaded, became overwhelmed with this feeling of not being good enough, and possibly took on the message that it had to really try hard to be good enough. Some people

> **The goal is to feel, I'm just as good as anyone.**

with states that are vaded in this way just give up and stop trying at all, becoming anti-social. Others spend their lives trying.

If you are a person who is not comfortable in your own skin, who does not think that you are okay, then you have at least one

Vaded state that has taken on this 'not OK' message and holds it on the inside. Even though there may be times that you think positively about yourself this underlying Vaded state will hang onto those feelings of not being good enough until it gets what it needs and is able to become a Normal state.

The good news is that moving a Vaded state to being a Normal state can happen. Even if it seems like your whole life you have not felt 'good enough' you can still get that relaxed 'I'm as good as anyone' feeling.

The goal is not to feel, 'I'm better than others'. It is for every Resource State to feel, "I'm just as good as anyone."

We all know there are multitudes of people who are better than us at practically every single thing we do. I once ran in the Sydney marathon. After training for months, after feeling that my body suited distance running, after doing all the right things to prepare there were still about a thousand people who finished in front of me. The thought went through my mind that this was one city in one country and if had I ran in any other city in the world there would have been multitudes finishing in front of me.

I thought how amazing the athletes are who win or get anywhere close to winning. They must have the body, the motivation, the temperament, the time, everything just right to be in that elite group. Still, I was very happy having done my run and having finished where I did. It would have been okay if I had finished last, or not finished at all. It would have been great to have finished first, or to have run the greatest run ever run. There is nothing wrong with fantasy. The bottom line is, I wanted to run.

I did, and I was glad I did. Parts of my physical body were not so glad, but that is another story.

The point of the marathon is that even though I did not come anywhere close to winning or to being in the front group I felt like I was just as good a person as anyone else in the race. I did not feel like I was any better, but I did feel that I was just as good.

Everyone is just a person, struggling along in their own life. To respect their struggle and our own struggle places us all in the same group. We are all different, but we are all strugglers. Some people have lives that are harder, possibly with less food, less clothes, and a broken body, and some people have lives that are easier, but we are all strugglers.

Depression and suicide increase when societies advance economically to where life is easier. It is the wealthier countries and families that have more 'bad feelings about self' so it is not what we have that gives us our self-concept. It may be that those who have to worry about where the next meal is coming from are focusing on surviving and are not focusing on, 'Am I good enough?'

Imagine yourself sitting in a crowd of people looking at those around you. If you feel some kind of hierarchy, like you are better than some, and some are better than you then it is likely that you are not at peace with who you are.

Obviously there are hierarchies, some are taller, some shorter, some are richer, some poorer, some are skinnier, some heavier, some are older, some younger, but each and every person has their own life and struggle. If you can look out and see equality you are probably at peace with yourself. It is the fear of not being good enough that creates the need to view others as better or worse.

If we are afraid we may not be good enough it can be safer to see some as less good. If we know we are as good as anyone, we gain the ability to respect others in their own skin. No one is a threat to us and no one is seen as less than us.

I remember a time when I was working on a Master's degree I had dinner with a man who had finished his masters and a woman who had finished her PhD. I had the thought that it was interesting that we were all at the same table, and I actually said that. I was showing my ignorance about how people are really all the same. It was a silly thing to say. It is better to understand that the best we can do is to respect everyone and to want to make situations easy for them, not to be concerned about how we look. If someone sees hierarchies it is because they feel insecure.

Steps to feeling positive about yourself

That feeling of 'I'm not good enough' can be real and palpable. A big thing to understand is that what we feel often has little to do with the moment. Don't get me wrong, moments can be highly related to what we feel. We can feel fantastic if things are going well and we can feel awful if things are not turning out the way we want, but it is often the case that what we feel does not really match the moment.

Why is it that we can feel alright, then see someone else who has better clothes, or see someone who looks down on us for some reason, then our feelings change and we feel awful? This change of feelings can happen in instant. Physically, the temperature hasn't changed and we are no hungrier than we were a moment before. Our bank account has not changed. We still have the same things to do during the day. What is it that gave us that sense of low self-esteem? What tender spot was touched? That tender spot that was touched is a Resource State that has taken on the feeling of not being good enough.

Having low self-esteem means we have a child Resource State that needs to feel love and support. This tender spot, this child Resource State that doesn't feel good enough, can quickly be brought to the surface by a critical look or comparison, and when it comes to the surface with its feelings of not being good enough we are filled with those feelings.

I will give you an example of what can vade a child Resource State in a way that makes it feel unlovable. A child desperately wants a loving connection with a parent. Sometimes parents are not in a position in their life to be able to show unconditional, accepting love. When a parent is not able to show love in an accepting and unconditional way it may be interpreted by the child as, "I am not lovable."

In truth, every child deserves unconditional love, and if a parent cannot show this to the child, it is the fault of the parent, not the fault of the child. It is not that the child is unlovable, it is that the parent is not able to show love at that time in life. Life is often difficult for parents, and they are not always able to be available in an unconditional and caring way. This is not the fault of the child. Children are able to show love.

A Resource State that feels unlovable can come out at any time. When that vaded part that feels unlovable finally gets what it needs, when it feels totally loved and accepted and supported then it can rest easily on the inside and allow us to respond to life situations in a way that we want.

When that part of us gets what it needs we can feel secure even when we know there are many others that are better than us at many things. When that part of us gets what it needs, we can do the things we want to do. We do not have to compete in an attempt to feel good enough. It is well worth making sure that part of us that has felt 'not good enough' gets what it needs.

Of course, it is possible that we may have more than a single part with feelings of not being good enough. That is okay. By learning how to assist one part in getting what it needs the same thing can be done to assist any other part.

It is important how you look at that fragile part of yourself. If you look at it with frustration or disdain, that is only going to make you feel worse.

Many people criticize their fragile parts. They say things like, "I hate myself when I'm like that." Or, "I am hopeless."

Imagine being a fragile child and hearing someone say that they hate you and that you are hopeless. That would not help that tender Resource State to feel safe and secure, loved and supported. It would actually make it feel less good and more hopeless.

We need to look at our fragile parts with love and support, like we might a small kitten that is frightened. Our fragile parts are really a gift to us. It would not be good to live life as a computer with no feelings and no sensitivity. It is our fragile parts that allow us to feel. They have a huge role to play for us and they can enrich our lives immensely. We can be proud that they are there.

The proper roles for our fragile parts are to be able to come to the surface when we feel safe and secure so that we can feel more deeply and enjoy our experience more fully. They are not best suited to come to the surface when we are being criticized. They are not best suited to come to the surface when we are being compared to someone else or when we compare ourselves to someone else. During these times it is better for them to stay below with the love and support of a nurturing Resource State. But, if we are with someone we feel safe with who gives us a hug and tells us that they love us it is truly wonderful to hear that with one of our fragile parts.

When you feel a low self-concept you have an opportunity to praise a fragile Resource State that has come to the surface. You have an opportunity to give it the message, "I'm really glad you're there. There are times I really need you to help me enjoy life more fully, but you don't have to be out for this. I want to take you down inside and give you the love, support, and honor that you deserve and that you have always deserved. At the same time, I want to invite a more intellectual or crusty, assertive Resource State to come out. I want a state out that fully knows that we are all equal in value. I want a state out that can respond in a way that I can feel positive about later."

Giving yourself this message does two things. It is the first step, a big step, in helping that wonderful tender part of yourself to understand how important and positive it is, and it also invites a Resource State out that is appropriate for the situation at hand.

Sometimes you may want a Resource State out, for example if you were being attacked, that is assertive and powerful. Whether you want a Resource State out that is good at making people feel good or one that is more assertive and powerful, it is important during these times that your wonderful fragile and tender states are respected and supported on the inside. This is not the time when they need to leave their safe and loving place inside.

You will need to be aware of parts of you that you may want to bring out. You can think of a time when you are very much in your head, thinking, times when you are not really feeling much. Maybe when you do math problems or plan the roads you will take on a trip are times when this thinking part is out. Knowing that you have this thinking part enables you to bring it out when you need it. Likewise, you might think about times when you have been assertive, when you have spoken to a friend or work colleague in a direct and non-emotional way. This assertive part of you can be used at other times too, just as your thinking Resource State can.

Here it is in a nutshell.

- You feel a surge of self-doubt or low self-esteem (this means that fragile Resource State has come to the surface, one that has not felt good about itself in the past).
- You may find that using the helping hand from chapter 5 is a good way to connect your helping state with your

fragile and sensitive state. Your understanding, nurturing Resource State internally takes it by the hand and tells it that it is wonderful and important and that it doesn't need to be out now. Your nurturing Resource State calls for another state to handle the present situation and takes the tender, fragile state inside where it can get the love and support and appreciation it deserves.
- A more intellectual or assertive Resource State comes to the surface to handle the present situation in a way that you will feel positive about later.

The more you know your Resource State resources the easier this will be for you. When you are aware of your parts you know they are there to be called to the surface.

Remember, for this to work best you need to understand how wonderful it is to have tender and fragile parts. Your understanding this is sending a message to your fragile and sensitive parts that they are good, honored, and important. This helps them understand their importance and it helps you experience the world in a positive way. When your Resource States feel important you have good self-esteem.

When your fragile parts learn to feel good about themselves they will no longer respond to the negativity at the surface. They will no longer be reminded of the negative messages that they have taken on in the past because they have grown to understand how wonderful and sublime they really are.

We can be thankful for our fragile states. Computers are handy, but we don't want to be one. Our fragile parts are the ones that feel the most. They are the ones that can most enjoy a sunset. They can most enjoy a hug. They can most enjoy the beautiful things in life. They are very important and very useful. When they come out, because they are sensitive, they can feel exposed. It is right to have them out when it is safe and it right to have intellectual or assertive states out when it feels less safe.

Chapter 16: Moving from mean behaviour to caring behaviour

Mean behavior is hard to understand. Why are people mean to each other? An interesting thing is that not only are people mean to each other, we can be mean to our own Resource States. One Resource State can disrespect, and react negatively to other Resource States. Being mean does not happen randomly. There are reasons.

People are mean for one of two reasons. They either feel disconnected from others and feel upset that they are not getting what is due to them, or they have a part that is mean simply because that is its role. Let's look at both of these two reasons why people are mean.

When we see others getting more than us, when we feel like we're not getting a fair share, when we feel we are not respected, it is easy to strike back. Striking back is often mean behavior.

It could be that the person with this kind of mean behavior really is not getting a fair share of what life has to offer, or it could be that this person is misinterpreting the share that is being received. Either way the person who is striking back feels disconnected and disillusioned. This person holds the feeling, "Life is supposed to be better and it is not." This feeling of not getting what is fair causes the person to feel disconnected and uncaring about their own behavior.

This person may not care who they hurt because they have stopped empathizing with those around them. They have stopped really knowing what it feels like to be cared for by others or to care for others.

It is sad that some people feel disconnected, unloved, and cold in their relationships with others. This is what allows one person to hit another without thinking about what it feels like to be hit. People can react this way even when they are receiving love from others, just because they have a child Resource State that still feels unloved.

The other reason people are sometimes mean is because they have developed a Resource State with a role to protect or to fight, even if that means 'mean' behavior. A child may be raised in a family where fighting back is a way of self-protection, or is a way of getting respect from others in the family. This fighting back behavior may be encouraged by family members. This fighting back behavior may be mean behavior.

So, we have two reasons why people conduct mean behavior:

1. The person feels life is not fair and, "I am not going to be fair." This person feels disconnected and unloved.
2. The person has developed a Resource State with a role to fight, even if that means being mean.

There is little we can do to change someone else's behavior. There is a lot we can do to change our own. It is sometimes hard to think about ourselves being mean, but somebody has to be doing it, and it may be us.

If we feel disconnected from others and feel like striking back no matter who it hurts then we are being mean. If we notice that we say and do things that are hurtful or harmful, then we are being mean. The question is, "Do we want to stop being mean?" We can stop if we choose to.

Those people who feel disconnected, and feel like striking back no matter who it hurts have Vaded Resource States. They have states that feel unlovable. They have states that are hurt, that have tried for love and have not been met with loving behavior. They have been left feeling cold and hopeless in regards to love. If this sounds like you then Chapter 5 may be able to help you feel lovable again.

Every one of our Resource States is here to help.

That cold, strike back, feeling comes from a Resource State that really wants love. Read Chapter 5 carefully, charge your loving and nurturing hand with unconditional positive regard so that when you feel cold and rejected, when you feel like striking back, you can bring this nurturing loving Resource State to support the child state that did not get the love that it deserved. When this part of you gets the love that has always been deserved, it will feel like loving, and it will be open to other Resource States to be positive and loving toward others.

If you have a Resource State that has been trained to fight back, sometimes in a mean way, this Resource State needs to be praised for its willingness and ability to help you, while at the same time it needs to learn to help you only at certain times.

Every one of our Resource States is here to help. They all have important roles, even those that seem like they get us in trouble. The Resource State that can be sharp and cutting can be seen as an asset to have at the right time. By looking at this Resource State as an asset and being glad that it is there that Resource State will be more willing to come out only when it is needed. It is like having a big strong relative standing in the back of the room. You may never really need him, but it is nice to know that he is there. And, his knowing that you are glad that he is there makes him feel good too.

The trick is to make sure that you have another Resource State to take on the role that the big strong internal relative used to do, when meanness happened. For example, you may need a Resource State that can tell people exactly how you feel in a nice way. Think about times when you have been able to do this, with a child, with a friend, or at work. Think about how it felt being able to say exactly what you wanted to in a nice way that was respecting who you were talking with. When you are aware of how this Resource State feels give it a name. You may want to call it something like, "Assertive," or "Strong." In the future you will be able to use this part of yourself to relate to others in a respectful way, and in a way that respects yourself too. Remember, you deserve as much respect as anyone else. In order to be a kind person we need to be kind to everyone, our self included.

Therefore, to summarize, we can eliminate our mean behavior by making sure Resource States that feel unloved, are loved, and by making sure that our Resource States that have abilities to protect can protect us at the right time, and our clear and assertive Resource States can express our opinions at other times.

When we feel positive on the inside we do not feel like being mean on the outside.

Chapter 17: Communication and the way we respond to others

A big part of living is communicating with other people. We often feel good about our day when we communicate well with others. Good communicators are liked more and feel better expressed. They also are able to better learn what others have to say. We all have Resource States that enjoy communicating and that are good at it. What we want to be able to do is to have those Resource States out when we want to communicate.

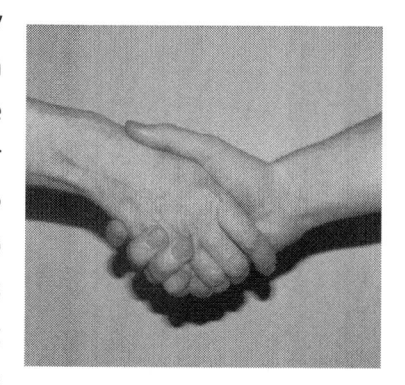

Our Resource States have a lot to do with our communication

There are two main ways we can improve our communication by helping ensure we are able to have the best communicating state out.

1. Our communicating state may be interrupted by a Vaded state that is overcome with nervousness or fear. If so, we need to heal this state.
2. We may not have our best communicator Resource State out when we try to communicate. If so, we need to find our best communicator state.

It is impossible for us to bring our best state out if a Vaded state jumps out when we want to communicate. Therefore, the first step in improving our communication is to make sure that any Vaded state that may have interrupted our ability to communicate the way we want gets the healing that it needs. Then, we will be able to look for the best Resource State for communication.

Vaded states and communication

Vaded states may cause us to freeze up and not be able to speak the things we want to say. They may even cause us to feel panic when we try to talk to some people, or try to talk to a group.

Here is what happens if a Vaded state is interrupting our communication. We start to talk to a person or to a group and we feel unable to say the things that we would like to say. We feel emotional and nervous, and we may feel that we could say something that would get us in trouble, or cause us to be judged.

The way to know if a Vaded state is interrupting our communication is merely to be aware if our nervousness or sense of being out of control is more than just the interest or excitement of the situation. It is normal to have some anxiety about speaking to a person or a group, but a Normal Resource State does not cause a flood of emotions to the level that it interferes with the ability to communicate. If you feel this flush of emotions that interfere with your ability to communicate then a Vaded state is most likely interrupting your communication.

What is appropriate is for you to be able to feel positive about your opportunity to share what you have to say, and it is appropriate to have a range of emotions from being totally relaxed to some feelings of tension. The tension you feel should not be more than heightened energy that gives you a better ability to communicate. Many comedians, actors, and speakers say they feel some anxiety before and during speaking, but the level of anxiety they feel releases enough adrenaline to give them more energy and not so much that it blocks their ability to communicate.

If a Vaded state is interrupting your ability to communicate you need to become aware of just exactly when this feeling comes to you, this sense of not being able to communicate. For example, if you are going to talk to a group, when is it that your nervousness starts? It may be right before you stand up to speak, it may be long before that when you are preparing to speak, or it may be when you actually get in front of a group. It may even be all of these times.

When you notice that high level of nervousness that means that a Vaded Resource State has come to the surface. You are experiencing that state's unresolved feelings from the past. This state needs to feel resolved, supported, and loved so that it can stay down below the surface and allow your best communicating Resource State to do its thing.

Remember, a Vaded state is like a small upset child. It needs safety and nurturance to feel OK. If it is disliked it only feels worse. The things you need to be able to help the Vaded state are:

- Be aware that the Vaded state has come out, and

- Use the techniques from Chapter 5 to nurture and heal the Vaded state.

If you prepare well using the techniques in Chapter 5 you will be ready to bring the resolution and support to this state as it comes out. That will free you to be able to bring your best communicating Resource State to the surface so you will be able to communicate in a relaxed and sharing way.

Here is an example. Paul becomes extremely anxious each time he talks to women who he would like to get to know better, or when he talks in front of a group. He has begun to think that he will never be able to communicate. Paul read Chapter 5 and prepares a helping hand with a nurturing Resource State, ready to bring support, nurturance, and love to any unresolved Resource State. He can prepare even several days before his Vaded state comes to the surface, or he can prepare even earlier on the same day.

Paul finds himself in a place where he can talk to a woman who he is interested in. He thinks about saying something to her and he feels a rush of anxiety that makes it difficult for him to speak. He recognizes that a Vaded Resource State has come to the surface, a state that is unresolved and that needs support. He understands that this is a good part of him that deserves support and love.

Paul is intellectually aware that he has his charged helping hand and that it is ready to bring support and nurturance to this Vaded state. He becomes aware of the part of his body where he most feels the Vaded state. It will normally be his stomach, chest, or head, but it does not matter where he feels it. He brings his helping hand to this part of the body, aware of the messages of unconditional love this hand holds. He presses the hand on to this part of the body making sure that that swirling amazing love is shared, allowing this state to feel the clearing and the loving hug. As he does this, Paul is aware that his nurturing state is bringing support and love to the smaller part of him that deserves and needs it. It is most important that Paul hold positive feelings toward this state, as it can feel what Paul feels.

Paul's anxiety quickly clears and he feels ready to bring out his communicative Resource State.

I can hear some of you thinking, "Paul's going to look really dumb putting his hand on his stomach." The length of time he will need to have his hand on his stomach, chest, or head is just a few seconds. It will likely go unnoticed, and even if it is noticed it will be much better for Paul to be ready to speak than for him to feel out of control, nervous and unable to communicate.

Making sure that a Vaded Resource State gets what it needs will help Paul communicate even if he does not do anything else. But, it will be much better for Paul if he can communicate from a state that is a good communicator. To make sure this happens Paul will have needed to identify his best communicating Resource State earlier. He only needs to learn his communicating Resource State once, and then he will be able to use that state to communicate for the rest of his life.

Finding and bringing out a good communicating Resource State

If we have the wrong state out we will not be able to communicate in the way we would most like. Here is how to find a Resource State that is a good communicator.

Think about a time in your life that you have communicated with someone in a relaxed and comfortable way. It may be when you were young having a sleepover. You may have been able to say exactly what you felt while wanting the person you're talking to to hear and understand. It may be at home while you are having a hot or cold drink with a friend or relative. It could be any time, but it is important to think about the specific time that you felt good about communicating with someone else. If you can't think of a time you feel good about communicating with someone else you can even think of the time you felt good about communicating with an animal, petting it and talking to it.

Think precisely about where you were when you were communicating well. What time of day was it? What was the lighting like? Who are you communicating with? How does your body feel? What kind of clothes do you have on? Think how exactly you feel as you place yourself at the time that you communicated well.

You have just brought out your communicating Resource State. What name fits this part of you that feels relaxed and comfortable communicating? Pick a name that fits this part of you, then using that name ask this part of you out loud if it will be willing to help you communicate in a relaxed and comfortable way when you want to communicate with others. Ask this part of you that enjoys communicating if it will be available to come out when you need it and want it. It will be able to come out as long as you have resolved any Vaded state or states that have previously interrupted your communication.

Let's say the name that you have given this part of you is, "Communicator." Communicator is a resource of yours. It is a great Resource State to have. It is part of you that can express what you want to say comfortably in a way that others can hear. Resource States like to have an opportunity to help. Communicator will enjoy helping you when you want to communicate. Be aware of what you feel like when communicator is out, of the skills communicator has, and how communicator is a resource of yours.

When you have prepared the helping hand to bring support and love to any Vaded state that might come out, and when you have become aware of your communicator Resource State you are ready to communicate well. You have both the resource to communicate and the opportunity to use that resource.

There is one more technique that can be helpful to you in communicating well. Sometimes you have a Resource State that is knowledgeable about a topic, but that Resource State may not be able to communicate what it knows very well. Now that you have become aware of a Resource State that communicates well, it is wise to introduce it to the part of you with the information that you want to communicate. This may sound a little funny, but it is easy to do.

Think about exactly what you want to say. Become aware of the information that you have that you want to share with someone else. When you do this you are bringing out the Resource State that has the knowledge. Give this part of you a name. Ask yourself, "What can I call this part of me that has this information?" When you get a name for this Resource State, ask it if it would be willing to share its information with your communicating Resource State when that Resource State is ready to communicate. Suggest internally that the two states have an internal handshake so that they will be able to share the information, and so that communicator will be able to have this information to share with others.

Both states should be happy with this internal sharing because it helps each state. The more you know your states the more empowered you become in using your resources.

> **If we hear someone being critical it is not good to be in a reactive state.**

Responding to someone who is critical

If we hear someone being critical of us it is not good for us to be in a reactive Resource State. It would be better for us to be in a state that can hear the criticism, assess it, and respond in an assertive way.

When we hear someone being critical of us it often brings out a Vaded state. If this happens the techniques above can be used to calm the Vaded state and to help normalize it.

It may be important to think about what kind of Resource State we want to be in when we hear critical information. An intellectual state that can assess what is being said with little feelings is probably a good state to be in when we hear critical information. An intellectual state can determine if what the person is saying has value. Then, with this intellectual understanding we can decide how we want to respond.

It may be that we will want to respond from an assertive Resource State, one that can say clearly what we want to say and also say it in a firm and straightforward way. This assertive Resource State may not be our communicator state, although it may be helped by that state.

If you do not know an assertive Resource State see the section, *Finding an Assertive Resource State* in Chapter 13, the chapter that is on Anger. This section demonstrates how to make sure you have an assertive state ready when it is needed.

You may want to introduce your assertive Resource State to your communicator Resource State so they can work together when you need to communicate in an assertive way. The more you practice these techniques the better you will get at them. It is good to be able to become aware of the Resource States that we have, and to be able to help them work together.

There is no reason why each of us do not communicate in the way that we would like. We may never be able to be a truly eloquent star, or a great comedian. Those people have built those gifted Resource States from childhood, but we can learn to say what we want in a clear and comfortable way. It is a gift to ourselves and to others to be able to express what we know and feel, and to be able to hear what others have to say.

Chapter 18: Health

How much does the way we think impact on our health? A lot.

There are many ways that the way we think changes us physically. There are also many things that are physical and cannot be changed by the way we think. Therefore, the answer to the question about how much the way we think impacts on our health is that it does impact on our health, but it does not totally define our health.

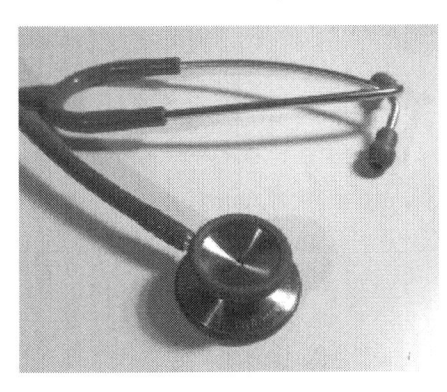

There appears to be a number of things that are purely physiological. I cannot change my height by changing the way I think. I cannot get rid of tooth decay by changing the way I think. I cannot grow back a limb by changing the way I think.

There are also a number of physical aspects of our bodies that are obviously tied to how we think. A tension headache is what the name implies, a headache caused by muscle tension. That muscle tension comes about from stress, in other words is caused by the way we think.

In psychology and medicine there is a thing called the fight flight syndrome. It is a good example of how the way we think physically impacts upon our bodies. Here is what happens. We are stressed by something. In response to the stress our bodies release adrenaline; also called epinephrine. This chemical creates a number of physiological changes in our bodies. Our heart rate increases, digestion slows down, the creation of antibodies slows down, blood flows slower into the hands and feet, our hair tends to stand up more, and we become physiologically stronger. These are all measurable physiological changes brought about immediately by stress.

The fact that stress slows down our production of antibodies means that if we are exposed to a cold or a flu during a time that we are stressed we may not have enough antibodies to fight it off. Therefore, people with more stress tend to get more colds and flu's.

A few years ago I was called as an expert witness in a case relating to a psychologist's use of hypnosis to increase the breast size of a client. In order to prepare for my cross-examination I read all the research I could find on hypnosis and altered breast size. I found it interesting that approximately 2/3 of the women who participated in this research had been able to increase their breast size by an average of 1 cup following the use of hypnosis. This was explained by breast size being related to hormonal secretions.

> **When Resource States achieve an internal peace it is easier to maintain a healthy body.**

Hypnosis was used to alter the hormonal secretions so that the female participants could alter the size of their breast without invasive surgery. Hormonal releases are affected by how we think. Adrenaline is also a hormone.

Biofeedback is a method of using instruments to give feedback to clients who are learning to alter stress levels, blood pressure, and even brainwave patterns. The patient observes the needle, a sound, or even plays a video game to learn to control the hormonal releases and stress levels of the body.

Often patients can have a positive impact upon their own health by changing the way they think. In the chapter on anger I discussed how learning to express feelings and deal with anger appropriately can have major impacts on our chances of getting cancer or coronary heart disease. Therefore, it is obvious that the way we think impacts upon our health.

A stressed person may sleep uncomfortably or in a physically twisted fashion. This can lead to backache. Stress has been associated with irritable bowel syndrome, warts, herpes, endometriosis, tension and migraine headaches, muscle pain, and many more physical manifestations.

The way we think can also lead to risk taking behaviors that can have physiological impacts upon us. Overeating, the use of drugs, and many more risk-taking behaviors are often the result of Resource States that are not at peace.

It is therefore easy to see that physiology is related to the way we think, even though there are aspects of physiology that are not. We may be genetically prone to some physical symptom but if we can stay relaxed and if our Resource States are comfortable, we may not ever manifest those symptoms. There are three categories relating to how we think and physiology.

How our minds affect our bodies

There are physical symptoms not related to the way we think, such as our height, tooth decay, and eye color.

There are physical symptoms that are caused by the way we think such as tension headaches.

There are physical symptoms that are not entirely caused by the way we think, but that can be impacted by the way we think.

When Resource States achieve an internal peace it is easier to maintain a healthy body. This does not mean that we will have bodies that do not age or bodies that do not get sick, but we will have bodies that do a better job of maintaining health than they otherwise would.

In my own experience, after learning to listen to my Resource States and help them to maintain a better internal peace I was able to go 14 years without having a cold or flu. Then I did get a cold and it reminded me how miserable they are. During that 14 years there were many moments I felt like I might get a cold. I felt the early warning signs of one.

When I felt these early warning signs I would sit down in a comfortable chair, relax myself, and send a message inside asking my Resource States what it was that they needed to be relaxed and comfortable and for me not to get a cold. I would listen, and then the message would come into my mind, usually something like you need more sleep, you need to eat better, you need to eat some hot chillies, or something else. I would send a message back to this Resource State that I would do what was asked of me and that I would appreciate not getting the cold. I would keep my bargain and as I said for 14 years this worked. I'm not sure what happened but the year swine flu came around I did get a bad cold. It probably had nothing to do with swine flu, but that was the year that I got the cold.

There is a range to the amount of physical ailments that our bodies will have. We have different predispositions to illness. If we keep our Resource States relaxed, comfortable, and help them get along with each other, that will help keep us at the lower end of the range of physical ailments that we might have.

In order to maintain better health, we need to help ensure that our Resource States are in a Normal condition, that is, they are not Vaded, Conflicted, or Retro. Following the steps in chapters 5, 6 and 7 will help maintain healthy, Normal Resource States.

If you do have a physical symptom that you think might be psychologically related it is a good technique to set down, relax yourself, and attempt to experience the physical symptom as much and as totally as possible. Then notice the emotion that you feel when engaging with that physical symptom, then use techniques in chapter 5 to bring healing to the emotional content of the physical symptom. It is sometimes the case that the physical symptom will disappear.

I will give you an example. I had a client who presented with some things she wanted to change. She happened to mention that a number of months earlier she had been in an accident and had since not been able to raise her arms above her shoulders. She said that her doctor and physiotherapist had told her that if she continued to do physiotherapy that in 18 months she should be able to raise her arms much higher. She said that she had completely healed from the accident but that she had just not recovered an ability to raise her arms above her shoulders.

During the session hypnotherapy was used to address the issue that she presented with. This issue had nothing to do with her arms. Before ending the hypnotherapy session I asked her to raise her arms as high as she felt comfortable in raising them. She raised both arms to shoulder height. I asked her, as she held her arms as high as she felt she could raise them, what emotion she noticed having. She said she felt emotionally constrained. I ask her if I could call this part of her that felt emotionally constrained, "Constrained" and she said I could.

I said (paraphrased), "Constrained, thank you for talking with me. Tell me more about how you feel right now." This Resource State that had been given the name Constrained did not speak with an adult's voice, but spoke with the voice of a frustrated child. I ask it how old it felt speaking in that voice. Then I ask it to go back to being that age, feeling constrained like it 'does right now', and tell me what was happening. This constrained Resource State told about being in a situation where she felt out of control, and unable to do what she wanted. She felt that it was not fair that she could not do what she wanted.

I told it that we know this isn't happening right now so you can say anything you want to this person who is saying you can't do what you want, and I encouraged this constrained Resource

State to speak out loud as it said what it wanted to. I then ask for another more mature nurturing Resource State to come to it and give it help, love and support, and I made sure that "Constrained" felt free and able to be in control of its inner space.

I asked it what it liked to do (play) and suggested that it would be able to do that on the inside and during appropriate time on the outside so that the adult could enjoy life that much more. I ask it how it felt after making these changes and it said it felt free. I suggested that now since it felt "Free" it might now like to be named Free, because the name 'Constrained' did not really fit how it feels any more. The Resource State was very happy to be named, "Free."

A few minutes later after the hypnosis session had finished and we had talked about the issue that had brought the client in, I asked, "Before you go would you just raise your arms one more time as high as they feel comfortable?" She raised her arms straight up over her head, elbows straight, with her hands reaching toward the ceiling. As she did this a look of surprise filled her face.

She had had a Resource State that had been vaded for many years. It felt constrained and it had constrained her muscles after the accident so they were not able to stretch out properly in a relaxed way. It is not unusual for Resource States to interact with our physiology in this way.

Mental health and physical health are closely tied. Being at peace internally allows the body an opportunity to heal, to straighten, and to be as healthy as it can be. Part of being free is being as physically healthy as possible. We can sometimes improve our physical health by improving our mental health. It is exciting that that is possible.

Chapter 19: Honesty

One might ask, "What does honesty have to do with Resource States and good mental health?" When a person has a level of honesty that all Resource States feel good about then there can be inner peace, but if a person is dishonest in one state, and then feels bad about it in another state, or feels confused about it then the dishonesty is a problem for the person and it is a Resource State problem. Also, dishonesty often interferes with social relationships and this can cause anxiety for all Resource States involved.

What is honesty?

This is a more interesting question that it at first may appear. Honesty may be seen like it would just be always telling the truth but there are a number of aspects to this that need to be considered.

- Is it dishonest to keep from telling someone something they have a right to know, but they do not ask?
- Is it sometimes better to lie?
- What type of honesty can a person feel good about?
- Can we be dishonest to ourselves?

Is it dishonest to not tell someone something they have a right to know, when they do not ask?

Yes.

Sometimes people are slippery and avoid telling the truth by answering questions in a way that technically are correct, but that avoid the real truth that the person would want to know. If someone is having an affair and not telling their partner then that is just as dishonest as point blank lying. Just because the partner has not asked, "Are you having an affair?" does not matter in terms of honesty. Deception is dishonest. If you know something that someone in your circle has a right to know and you do not tell them then you are holding a lie. That is deception and it is dishonest.

Deception is taking place if you are someone who has a relationship to the person who is being deceived where they would hope for you to come forward with the truth. For example, if you become aware that a neighbor down the street is being lied to by their partner and you do not have a relationship with that neighbor where they would feel hurt if you did not come forward with the information you know, then it is not dishonest to stay out of their business. You cannot go around telling everyone everything you know about their lives and it would not be appropriate to do so.

If you are a part of the dishonesty (for example, if you are the person their partner is sleeping with) then you are being dishonest. If you are part of the lie, then it would be honest to demand that the uninformed person be told or tell them yourself.

I knew a woman who was having an affair with a man who had a partner who was not being told. The woman thought she was innocent because she was not directly lying to anyone. The person who poisons the food is just as guilty as the person who delivers it.

Do unto others as you would hope them to do unto you, and you would not want anyone to be a part of a conspiracy against you. You would want them to see that you were treated with honor, even if you had never met. Living with honor makes it easy to be honest and that makes it easy for our Resource States to respect each other. That helps give us inner peace.

So, if you know something about a person you are close enough to that they would expect you to tell them then it is only honest to tell them. If you are a part of a deception even if you have never met the person it is honest to make sure they are no longer deceived.

Is it sometimes better to lie?
Yes.

It is not better to lie for selfish reasons, but it is sometimes better to lie for loving reasons, and the decision about when it is better to lie needs to be made very carefully. It is not good to use the excuse that they would be better off not knowing if the real reason we don't want to tell the truth is a selfish one.

There are loving lies.

Here is an example of a loving lie. In World War II if you were hiding a Jewish family upstairs when a member of the Gestapo came to your door and asked if you had seen any Jews it would have been more loving to lie, "No, I have not seen any." Lying in that instance is not selfish, you could actually be getting yourself in trouble by lying. It is loving. You are saving lives and you are preventing someone from committing a travesty.

I know someone who has Alzheimer's. After contracting Alzheimer's her son died. For many months she would ask where he was, and she would continue to ask questions about why he was not there. At first, her daughter told her each time she asked that he had died. Each time the woman heard that her son had died she became very distressed. To her it was like hearing about it for the first time. Her daughter decided that it was more loving for her to not answer her mother's questions with the truth. Rather than put her mother through the agony of finding out that her son had died over and over again she decided it was more loving to tell her something else.

There are many examples, but they all come down to asking yourself in a selfless way, "What is the most ethical thing for me to do? What is right? What will I feel good about on my final day of living?

I said above that it is dishonest to keep from someone a truth, even when they do not ask. If you see someone who you believe is ugly, it would not be good to go to them and tell them, "You are really ugly," even though you believe it. The little girl who loves her Bullwinkle cap and is enjoying the experience of wearing it should not be told, "You look ugly in that," even if that is what you think. Let her enjoy her experience. That is not hurting anyone, and there is no value in ruining her day.

At a restaurant a waitress once asked me, "How old do you think I look?" I could see she felt really good about believing that she looked younger than her age. Her eyes told me that. I under-guessed her age and everyone was happy. It was a loving lie.

What we need to be careful about is using the concept of a loving lie to deceive in a non-loving way. It would not be good for someone to be having an affair and lie to their partner about it, excusing the lie by saying, "It would be too hard on her to know." That is a selfish lie where you are getting a payoff from the lie. The person who does that is deceiving to get something they want. A selfish lie can hurt others and can create internal conflicts in the person who is lying.

You tell your partner you are taking them home for an early night to bed, knowing that friends are there for a surprise birthday party. It is a loving lie and the person you told loves you for it.

What type of honesty can a person feel good about?

There are two things to think about to feel good about honesty, the external and the internal. The external is the other people and the internal is inside us, our Resource States. Everyone may not be happy if you tell the truth. For example, if someone else is involved in your lie they may not feel good about you telling the person who has a right to know. They may try to convince you to lie or to deceive.

It is your decision whether you are honest, not the decision of someone else who is dishonest. In the end, you are not helping a person by making it easier for them to maintain a lie. Think about being the person who would be lied to. If you would like to be told the truth, if you feel you would have a right to be told the truth, then it would be appropriate to tell the truth.

This brings the focus to the internal. What will we feel like on the inside? Will we have Resource State conflict on the inside if we lie? We need to help Resource States find a level of honesty that all Resource States can accept and feel good about.

It feels great on the inside when all our states can come to an agreement that all can live with. That does not mean that all Resource States will want to abide with behavior that allows us to be honest. It can be tempting to do things that we would not want to tell someone about.

It might be tempting to steal someone's money that is left on the table. It would obviously be dishonest to deceive them. One Resource State might want the money, might think about what could be bought with it. One Resource State might offer reasons why it would be right to take it; "It would not be missed," and another Resource State might say, "It is not mine and it is wrong for me to take it." It is only when the Resource States can respect each other and all agree with the decision that internal harmony can be the experience.

It is necessary to learn to think ahead so we can live in the way that will keep us out of Resource State conflict about lying. We need to learn to think about being honest with those in our inner circle when we decide to put ourselves in certain situations. Think about living in a way where you will not have to withhold any information from those who trust you. Think about living in a way that you can be proud of later.

What if someone asked you to come up to their motel room? Even if you know that it is innocent, if this is something that would be impossible to be truthful about to your partner then it would be better to say no.

Learn yourself. Do not put yourself in a situation where you may do something that would be hard for you to be honest about. By thinking ahead you can live in a way that is easier to be honest. This does not mean that you should live a life that is not one you choose.

Generally, you need to be able to live the life you choose as long as you feel that it is an ethical way to live. If you feel too constrained by someone else it may be that you need a different type of relationship with them, or you need to go ahead and live your choice, be honest with them, and leave their growth up to them.

It is OK, though, for you to compromise what you would like to do with how it would make someone else feel. It is wonderful to respect others and compromise, it is just not good to consistently live the life that is not your own. Just be true to yourself and be honest.

Some people have been living with lying for a long period of time, possibly a lifetime. It may take some time for these people to arrive at a level of truth that they can respect internally, that all their states can respect.

Those who have a right to know

People have a right to know something if it directly affects them and they need that information to make informed decisions about their life. A person has a right to know if the trust they have placed in another person is misplaced. A person has a right to know information about their own health. A person has a right to know information that would lead them to make wise business choices.

One of the things I regret is not telling a person I felt close to something they had a right to know. We had been in an intimate relationship, and when we split she asked me to promise her that I would not start a relationship with a woman she knew. I hardly knew the person, and I made the promise. When I made the promise I was honest in my promise. Then, a few weeks later my work brought that other woman and myself together and I found myself wanting to know her better. What went through my head at the time was, "My ex should not be able to dictate who I see. I should be able to see anyone I want because we are no longer together." I started a relationship with the other woman and did not get that information to my ex, who I had no direct contact with any longer. Later, she found out that I had broken my promise to her, was hurt, and I felt really bad about hurting her by breaking my promise.

I should not have made the promise in the first place, but after I did, if it was a promise I decided was not appropriate I should have contacted my ex and explained that I should not have made the promise, I should have apologized for doing so, and I should have told her I was going to see the other woman. I would not have felt guilty had I done that. Guilt is a heavy feeling and one we should live in a manner to avoid.

Those who you should tell

If a person has a right to know information, and you have that information should you tell them? You should if you are close enough to them that they would expect you to tell them given your level of friendship. You should tell them if you are involved in the deception even if you do not know them or have never met them. It is a lie to not tell someone something they have a right to know. We all understand that. That is why we feel guilty if we are keeping something from a person close to us about what we are doing.

Those who you do not have a responsibility to tell

There are often times you may learn information about a person who would have a right to know, but that person is not in your circle and you have no relationship to the deception. In this case it is often best to stay away from the situation. If a member of a family confides in you that a person in their family is dying and has not been told, you do not have a responsibility to go to that person and tell them. If a friend confides in you that she is having an affair and has not told her husband, while it would be better to encourage her not to live a lie, it is not your responsibility to tell her husband unless he is also a friend of yours.

I do not advocate telling a mentally disturbed person something that would make them do something crazy. I do advocate creating a distance, if at all possible, from a dangerous person so you can live an honest life in a way that fits your philosophy.

Those who do not have a right to know

People do not have a right to information if they would make unethical use of that information, or if they are not mentally mature enough to make reasonable decisions with that information. If you know where a gun is hidden in the house and you know that a person with Alzheimer's would like to have that gun you should not tell them. They might do something with the gun that would be inappropriate. This is the same as if the Gestapo agent asked where a Jew is hiding. You should not tell him because he would do something unethical with that information.

Parents often know many things that they would not want to tell a two-year-old child. They know that the two-year-old is better off not having information of certain types. It is most loving to withhold information from people who do not have the mental development to be able to use that information appropriately. Still, we must be careful not to use this rider just to be selfish in some way. Anytime we lie we are showing a level of disrespect, because if we have made a decision that the person is too young or not able to use the information safely (Gestapo), then we are making a judgment against them.

Can we be dishonest to ourselves?
Yes.

If one Resource State is out and in control and says, "It is OK to eat that" knowing that other Resource States will be upset about it later, then we are being dishonest with ourselves. Chapter 7 is about being able to be internally respectful and honest.

What it takes to have Resource State peace about honesty
If we attend to the things above it is simple to feel good about honesty. It may be simple but it may take a period of time

to achieve. Old habits can die slowly. Here are the elements to achieving Resource State peace in regards to honesty.

You must have an idea about what honesty means to you. This way you have clarity, something to aim for that your Resource States can agree upon. I have suggested above that honesty is telling those people in our circle what they have a right to know. It may mean telling them things that would be hurtful to them, but there are rare times when it is most loving to lie, when it is unselfish and not self-serving. Keeping a truth from someone who does not ask, or who does not ask in the right way, is not being honest.

You must be an ethical person. Being an ethical person means you put what you feel is right above your personal selfishness. Think about what is right, as if looking at the situation from the perspective of a kind person outside that situation, then you can get an idea about what is right. Living that idea is being honest. It may be helpful to think about what an ideal person would do. That shows you what you think is right.

You need to be honest both to other people and to your Resource States. You cannot feel settled on the inside if one Resource State does something or says something that other Resource States cannot accept. Therefore, you must help your Resource States respect each other and learn to compromise in order to be an honest person, and in order to feel an internal peace.

By gaining an ethical idea about what is honesty and by living your ethics you can feel good about yourself. In other words your Resource States can feel good about each other. You will be able to sleep at night with a straight back. It is worth it.

Chapter 20: Sex

What an amazing subject. There are so many things that could be said about sex and so many different meanings to the word. This chapter will be about sexual activity:

- the things that allow us to feel comfortable during sexual activity,
- the things that in the past have kept us from feeling comfortable,
- the difficulty some people have in being honest about sexual activity and sexual identity,
- and the inner healing that will allow us to enjoy sexual activity in an honest and relaxed way.

When sex is referred to in this chapter I am talking about consensual adult sex. The sex I am talking about is that which can be enjoyed guilt free.

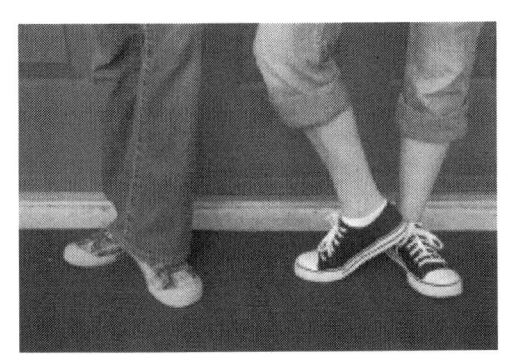

There is probably no other topic that peaks our interest as much as sex. There is probably no other topic that causes people to feel so much guilt, uncertainty, and fear than sex. Without sex our species would die out. Without our sexual drives movies, books and magazines would not be as popular, and without sex life would be much less interesting.

Physically, healthy sex feels fantastic. Being aware of someone who is sexy is stimulating and produces many positive feeling endorphins. Therefore, sex is good. So why is it that there is so much negativity wound up in thinking about and experiencing sex?

Let's look at sex a little bit from the outside before we go into our Resource States to find out what is going on inside. Sex preserves our species. It feels good, and we have a drive for sex so powerful that around the world babies continue to be made, often without the planning of their parents. The sexual drive is very strong.

The fact that it is difficult to go against the sexual drive gets a lot of people in trouble. Sex often occurs outside committed relationships, and sex often results in pregnancies that are unwanted and it often results in the spread of disease.

There is nothing unnatural about wanting to have sex. President Jimmy Carter, one of the most religiously conservative presidents, admitted that he had lusted for women other than his wife, Roselyn, although he did not act on it.

There is actually something unnatural about not wanting to have sex. If we are to celebrate being human and being in this amazing place, living in this amazing body, then it is natural to celebrate our human drives and the sensations that are experienced from responding to those drives. It is our choice how and when we respond to those sensations and it is good to do so in a healthy way so our bodies, our hearts, and our minds can all feel good.

Healthy sexual adjustment

What does it mean to have a healthy sexual adjustment? I have said throughout this book that good mental health relates to our Resource States achieving a Normal state, where each state has a role that is helpful to the person both internally and externally, and where each state respects and appreciates the other Resource States. This is true also with healthy sexual adjustment.

If there is a stressful inner conflict between the states regarding sex then there is no healthy sexual adjustment. When I say an inner conflict I am talking about Conflicted states that are disrespecting each other, or not liking each other to the point that it is a problem for the person.

There will always be Resource States that disagree, and that is appropriate. President Carter had Resource States that disagreed. One of his states felt 'lust' and another state was clear that, "We are not going to go there." The Resource State that felt lust said, "Yes," and another Resource State realized and accepted that Resource State as normal, but said, "No."

One person might have a state that admires and likes private jets, but that person would likely have a state that would accept the desire, but say, "No, we cannot afford that." There is a difference in opinion, but not a stressful conflict.

To make wise decisions it is helpful for Resource States to put their point of view forward. What is not helpful for us is when states disagree to the point that causes us high anxiety and inner turmoil, or when it causes us to do things that later we very much regret doing.

Healthy sexual adjustment is when each of our states has the right to express itself internally, but where there is also a system of internal compromising so that our actions are later viewed as appropriate. Healthy sexual adjustment is when we are able to feel positive about our sexual desires and only act on them in a relaxed and enjoying way when our states come to the agreement that it is appropriate. Healthy sexual adjustment is when our states have had any needed healing so that irrational fears or anxieties are not present.

Imagine having sex, feeling relaxed, feeling guilt free, feeling touch, feeling the bonding, and feeling free. There is no reason why, if we are lucky enough to find a person who we desire and feel guilt free being with, that we cannot have this type of sexual activity.

What keeps some people from enjoying sex?
There are two things that can interfere with a person's ability to enjoy sex and feel good about it afterward. They are:

1. Inner conflict can give us confusion and guilt in matters related to sex.
2. Vaded Resource States can come out around sexual activity and cause us to feel out of control with negative feelings.

Related to these two things is our need to have an opinion about sex that allows us to enjoy sex and feel good afterward. This can be challenging because many different religions and philosophies vary on ideas about sex.

Some religions hold that it is only appropriate to have sex to procreate. That means that followers of these beliefs are instructed not to have sex at all unless they are trying to have a baby. Priests in some religions are told that for them to have sex would be a sin.

This book is not about religious philosophy. Given the thousands of religious beliefs it would be arrogant for me to propose that I have the right one. A person's religious philosophy is part of that individual's ability to feel good about themselves and about the natural sex drive.

There is no question that it is OK to have a sex drive, to want to have sex. It is totally normal. I believe that religions that tell followers to abstain from sex even with spouses, have taken on those rules because many people have had difficulty learning to live with sex truthfully and honorably. Rather than attempt to define and educate appropriate sexual behavior some religious leaders have merely said, "No sex." It could also be that they have taken on these "no sex" beliefs because venereal diseases were seen as a message from a higher being.

As I cannot and should not define when is appropriate for someone to have sex, I will discuss how an inner compromise between states will allow individuals to feel okay about what is right for them.

People who see their sex drive as natural and who have a pathway within their philosophy to enjoy sex find it easier to obtain an inner Resource State peace. That is not a statement that means the way they think is the right way, just that both an acceptance of the sex drive and a willingness to physically respond to the drive reduces inner conflict.

Physiologically, it is easier to feel relaxed and comfortable if the sex drive is met with sexual climax, either with another person or alone. Physiologically, it is easier to feel satiated if when we feel hungry we eat, and it is no different with the sex drive.

Those people who accept that it is okay to either have sex with another person or to masturbate are better able to maintain a physical comfort than those who believe otherwise.

Let's say you belong to the group that feels it is OK for consensual adults to have sex at the right time, or for a single adult to masturbate. If you are in this philosophical group your body thanks you. You are able to quench your sex drive. Still, you may be confronted with a body that sometimes wants sex and a mind that says this is not the right time, not the right person, or not the right place.

Those people who believe that they should not have sex will have their physiological bodies against them. This is not to say that they are wrong, but it is to say that they may find following their beliefs more difficult. We are all the product of thousands of generations that had sex. Not one of our thousands of grandparents had no sex, so we naturally have a sex drive.

Both the sex, 'yes', group and the sex, 'no', group will have sexual urges that can cause inner conflict.

Inner conflict and sex
It is impossible not to have inner conflict relating to sex. It is something we all experience. The body says 'yes' and a Resource

State says, 'no'. There is nothing wrong with this. It is important for us to accept that our bodies have a natural desire for sex. We can be proud of having healthy, natural bodies. It is up to us to determine when, if ever, we want to respond to the body's natural desire for sex.

The section on honesty, Chapter 19, highly relates to this topic. We can only have Resource State peace if we live in a way that we are able to be honest. This honesty is both external and internal. It is good to be able to be honest with others, and it is also good to be honest with our internal Resource States.

If we feel we are not being honest, that is a Resource State that is not happy. Therefore, we need to feel that our sexual behavior matches our philosophy so we can be honest with ourselves, and we need to make sure we are being honest with others. "Getting away with it" is never possible, because if we feel dishonest we are not getting away with it within ourselves. We need to respect ourselves highly and make sure what we do is something that we can be proud of on our final day.

There are many different opinions about what kind of sexual behavior is right. It is common for individuals to change what they feel and believe is right, and that is appropriate. If someone were wrong and could not change that would not be good. For example, a person might have been taught that masturbation is bad, and then change to the opinion that it is good. During the time they are changing their opinion they will experience confusion. There is nothing wrong with confusion, but it is always better, even with our confusion, to do our best to be honest with ourselves, and to do what we feel is right.

When a person is dishonest with a partner regarding sex it is normal for them to feel guilt and inner conflict. The sexual drive can be very strong, and there may seem like there is no other way than to be dishonest. It is better to end a relationship before starting another. Some people attempt to have 'open' relationships where they tell their partner they are having sex with another person. This is very difficult.

There is something archetypal about sharing bodies in an intimate way that confirms the specialness of a relationship. It sends the message that, 'It is you and me' and no one else is special in this way. I have met people who say their open relationship is good, but I have not met anyone who continues to say that over a period of time. These relationships almost always fail.

It is interesting to note that people in fundamentalist religious groups tend to have better sex lives. It may be due to the trust and security they have in their relationships. Statistically, they have more sex than the rest of the population.

Vaded states and the ability to enjoy sex

This section relates to our emotions and fears that may keep us from enjoying sex. Some people have real fear and anxiety around sexual activity. Sex is a natural thing and it is natural to enjoy sexual experiences, given the inner peace spoken of above that comes with honesty with others and with our own philosophies, and given that we do not have a Vaded state that comes out with its unresolved emotions.

I have had clients who came to me after not having had sex in their marital relationships even after many years. They wanted to be able to have sex, and did not feel there was anything wrong with it, but they had fears that kept them from being able to participate in sexual activity.

Remember a Vaded state is one that has feelings that do not fit the present situation, so when someone has prohibitive fears around something as natural as sex, they are dealing with a Vaded state. There is a part of them that has experienced something in the past (it does not have to be something related to sex, although it may be, that comes to the surface and keeps them from enjoying sex.

We have seen that Vaded states can be resolved. They are states that are carrying an illusion that the past is still present and that what was frightening or what felt unloving in the past is still here and now. It isn't. If you have fears or anxieties around sexual activity you can use what you have learned in Chapter 5 to attend to the inner state that is upset. Know that these upset feelings are coming from a part of you that is worthwhile and needs nurturance, and when it gets the respect and nurturance it deserves it will allow your Normal sexual part to be in the moment.

As soon as you feel any fears or any level of being upset around sexual activity follow the steps from Chapter 5 to nurture the part that feels upset. With understanding and kindness press the right hand down and remember the loving support of 'Helper', like being a baby held by a truly loving person. Give an internal thank you to this wonderful part of yourself for accepting the hug and settling back internally while your loving physical part enjoys the present moment with your partner.

The more you practice this the better you will become at it, and the more nurturing the Vaded state will receive. It will become a Normal state, no longer vaded, and your fears around sex will be a thing of the past.

Remember, this process of working with and healing Vaded states is only for Vaded states. If your sexual issue is guilt because you are having sex at a time when you do not feel it is right, the issue is not a Vaded state. The issue is a Vaded state only when the emotion does not fit the situation.

Like our ability to enjoy the beauty of nature, the taste of amazing food, and the peaceful smile of a loved one, enjoying sex is a natural thing. It is appropriate for us to enjoy physical intimacy with someone we care about when we can have inner peace about this experience.

Chapter 21: Meet some of your states

Each time we change Resource States there is a change in how we feel, and how we relate to the world. It might be interesting to experience what some of our different Resource States feel like. We do not all have the same states, but most of us have the states that will be illustrated. We have many more states than these. The more aware we are of the states we have the more we will be able to use them when we choose. The more aware of the states we have the better we know ourselves and the better we can define how we want to be at different times.

Fragile

About it

All of us have fragile states. They are wonderful. They help us experience life in a way that uses our senses. We need to make sure it is safe for them to be out, but when it is safe they can allow us to taste, to feel, and to experience beauty.

Feeling it

It would be nice to be a child and be wrapped in loving arms. It would feel good being cuddled and held in a loving safe way at a time where we can truly relax. It is nice to remember a food that we truly enjoy and making the mouth full with it. It is really nice when someone gives us a special treat that we love to eat. It is nice to be amazed at lights and moving things.

How you feel now

How do you feel now? It is usually a good feeling. Our fragile parts are great parts. When they are brought out at the right time they make life enjoyable. We need to learn to bring them out when it is safe and let other parts help when it is not.

Angry

About it

We all get angry and it is a natural emotion. Often we have a state that can get angry, that has a role to protect a fragile part of us, especially if that part has been hurt.

Feeling it

Remember a person who bullied you. Remember the look on the bully's face. It does not feel good when someone much bigger picks on us or makes fun of us. It is wrong that bullies are really big. Just leave me alone. I hate being in a place I can't get out of and a bully is picking on me. It is really upsetting. I just wish they would go away and leave me alone.

How you feel now

When we are in an angry state we usually have some adrenaline flowing. It is like we want to lash out, whether we can or not. Our anger states are often our protectors, which is great, as long as we are happy with when they are out. Assertive states can protect too.

Depressed

About it

We all can feel depressed. When we are depressed it can seem like our whole life is depressed. If it is continuing and chronic it can be debilitating.

Feeling it

It's not good when things don't work out. To have something we really want, really care about and then it's gone. It feels like being inside a hole with big tall walls all around it. The air is not good and there's nothing that can be done about it. I just want to sit in the corner and not move. It feels like other people are getting on with their lives and that is somehow 'out there', not part of this silent low place.

How you feel now

Sorry about that. It is a very different feeling than the fragile feeling, isn't it? When we are fragile, and loved there is a real positive energy that we can use. Love is our next feeling. Feelings are not Resource States, but it is often the case that when we experience a feeling we go into any state that is experienced with that feeling, therefore we normally change Resource States when we have a big change in feelings.

In Love

About it

Most people would agree that being in love is a good feeling. We can be in love with different things, a person, a pet, a taste, a rainbow. It is fantastic to be open to those positive feelings when we are able to experience something we really like.

Feeling it

Imagine seeing a small kitten that has recently opened its eyes for the first time. It is so small you can hold it in your hand. It is fluffy and really likes being petted. When you do, it nuzzles and purrs.

Love

The flow of music fills the air,
The one you like is standing there.
A touch of wind has tipped the trees,
The smell of spring is in the leaves.
A smile so faint it's barely seen,
Tells of the love there is between.
Reflection of a distant wing,
Takes up its place in everything.
The sun peaks through a floating cloud,
To touch the words you speak aloud,
"It's not a thing I often say
but love is what I feel today."

How you feel now

Love is a light feeling. Life should be filled with light feelings. It is a feeling of really being where you are, being happy being where you are and feeling pure and positive about what is about you. When the clutter is gone love is there and can be felt. Being in a positive 'here and now' allows a vision of loving everything.

Smart

> **We each know better than anyone else what it is like to be us.**

About it
It is nice to be able to figure something out. There are different levels of smartness, and different things that people are smart about, but we are all smart in our own ways. We each know better than anyone else what it is like to be us.

Feeling it
Imagine doing a problem that is easy for you to do. It takes some thinking, and some time, but the process is not difficult for you. Imagine thinking about the best way to go to someone's house. Is it better to take a shortcut or go the longer way? Think about being given enough money to buy groceries for a week. You will need to think about what types of food you're going to buy, and how much it will cost for them.

How you feel now
You probably don't feel a lot right now. You don't need to when you calculate things. Our thinking state is very useful. It would be difficult to get along without it. When we are in it we don't feel much. It often uses the process of deduction to help us figure things out. These are all good states, and we can use them.

Reactive

About it
Sometimes we are in a state that is reactive. We know what it feels like to be in that state, because when another person is talking to us it feels like we are ready to feel bad about what they say.

Feeling it
OK, here it comes. He's going to criticize me again. He doesn't think I can do anything right. Nothing I do is right, no matter how hard I try. Why do I try? It won't be good enough. If he says one more word I am going to bite his head off. I'm not even going to let him get started. Who does he think he is, anyway?

How you feel now
You may feel a bit breakable or unbreakable, and defensive. It is not a good, light feeling. It is a protected feeling. Often the parts that feel defensive need nurturance, and help from assertive states to deal with what is happening. There is a role for each Resource State.

Athlete

About it
Sometimes when we compete in a sport we feel awkward, and sometimes we feel like we are 'in the groove'. It feels good to be doing something physically and feel like we know what we are doing, and feel like we are doing it well.

Feeling it
Think about a time when you have really enjoyed moving quickly and doing something physical. It could just be running at a

playground, going down a slide and running around to go down it again. If there is a sport you like to participate in, you might remember when you were really doing it well. It is a good feeling to feel the body do what we want it to do, almost automatically. There is a feeling of energy and fun. There is a mindless focus on just letting the body do what it really can do.

How you feel now

You may feel some energy. This state uses adrenalin in a good way to help the body to move. If you get in the right state you will be able to do your best at physical activities.

Spiritual

About it

Regardless of our beliefs, we all have times when the spirit feels free. There are moments where we intuitively sense that what is around us is amazing and beautiful. It is not a calculation. It is a feeling, an awareness.

Feeling it

Sometimes seeing a short string lets us better understand what a long string is. Think about being in a grey painted room with no windows and a low ceiling. There is no furniture, other than the chair you are sitting on. What does it feel like sitting in that room?

Now, think about safely standing near the edge of a sheer drop that goes down a few hundred feet, in front of you in the distance are mountains and below a valley and a lake. There is a real expanse that allows your senses to stretch while you take it in. The sky is filled with a golden iridescent sunset. You can see birds soaring below. One of the planets is already visible in the sky to the right.

How you feel now
Can you feel the sense of stretching out, of taking in what you see? Can you feel a lightness of spirit that was not there in the grey room? This is a great sensing state that helps us appreciate the amazing things we experience. This is a state that we can acknowledge and develop so we can get more benefit from experiences.

You can feel it around people. If you focus on a person facing away from you, who you have never met, you can get an intuitive feeling about that person.

When I was teaching at a university I once walked into an empty classroom with another person. She said, "I don't know what just happened in here, but it really feels negative in this room." I had already felt it even before she said anything. I walked around to the office and asked about it. There had been a meeting in that room that had just ended where a bad conflict had left people feeling hurt and negative. It left the room feeling negative too.

Allowing ourselves to be open to senses gives a further dimension to living. People who are good at this are often called intuitive.

Relaxed

About it
Relaxing is our fuel stop. The person who does not relax runs low on energy, is less creative, less productive, and more prone to

illness. Our state that is good at relaxing is an excellent resource and one we gain benefits from when we use it.

Feeling it

Imagine being in a bath with hot water just right in temperature. The water covers your skin, except your head. The water loosens your muscles so you can let everything go. You may have a candle lighting the room and you are there during a timeless time. Your arms float on the water. You watch them to see just exactly how still they become when you release all you muscles in the hot water. You close your eyes and listen to the sound of lying in the warm water.

How you feel now

When we deeply relax our muscles feel like they have been put back on the shelf for a while. Some of them can stay there while we use others. Often our bodies are hungry for rest. It is good to feed them, and when we do there is a peace. To have that peace our other states need to recognize the importance of re-energizing by relaxing.

Dreams

I want to fly,

lie on a lullaby,

close my eyes,

and let the world go by.

I want more than sight and sound

and touch and feel.

I want to be a part of something real.

The senses tell of things to me,
but all comes secondhandedly.

I want to flow
and be
and grow,
and know the parts of things there are to know.

I want to fly,
lie on a lullaby,
melt inside,
and ride, and ride, and ride, and ride.

Chapter 22: Enjoyment

It is time to look at the top half of the glass. I want to talk about what we can do after we have taken care of our major issues. We often focus on how to fix something that is giving us a problem. This makes sense because if something is giving us a problem it is hard to keep from focusing on that, and that can keep us from enjoying what is around us. Therefore, before we can really enjoy life it is important to attend to our major issues first. Much of this book is about how to do that.

Once we have moved our Vaded, Retro, and Conflicted states to Normal states we can focus on enhancing our enjoyment. The world in which we live is one of many wonders. The different colors, shades, plants, animals, relationships, and our different senses are here to be enjoyed and appreciated.

Imagine being in a flat suburban lot with a high solid fence surrounding it. It is not a very interesting place, especially if there are annoying things in that lot that demand your attention.

Now, imagine at once being OK with everything around you and being at a mountain vista looking out at other mountains in the distance, with grassy valleys below leading into wooded gullies. There are birds flying and everywhere you look holds something interesting and beautiful.

Imagine how your spirit feels there stretching out into the distance, exploring the depth and the plethora of places and colors before you. Feeling your spirit stretching can be awe-inspiring when we are open to the experience. It is possible for things that were annoying in the past to be seen from a new prospective.

After using the body to the point that it is tired and hungry, imagine eating food that is just right, that is full of flavor and that the body absorbs immediately. Imagine being open to think about from where that food has come, how it has been grown and prepared and the taste and nourishment it provides.

Imagine being relaxed and physically touched in a loving way by another person, and imagine touching the other person in a loving way while feeling safe, honest and accepted. Imagine learning something that is new and amazing to you, that you had not known before but that you are really glad you know.

Imagine seeing a friend or relative that you had not seen for some time and that you are really grateful to be able to see and catch up with, and they are grateful to catch up with you. Imagine sitting on the couch at the end of the long useful day feeling yourself able to rest deeply and have some 'time out' either quietly or with a conversation, a book, a favorite TV show, or a movie.

What it takes to enjoy

These imaginings can go on and on. There are many wonderful things about living, when we are ready to appreciate them from our Normal states. The key to appreciating them and enjoying them is to make sure that we have the right Resource

State out each time, a state that can really appreciate what is happening in the present.

If you are a person who likes a piece of chocolate it would be a waste for you to chew up and swallow that piece of chocolate while you are busy doing and concentrating on your taxes. The intellectual, mathematical, concentrating state that would be out doing taxes is probably not the state that can best enjoy a piece of chocolate. If you are going to have a piece of chocolate you might as well do it right. Pause, and invite a state into the conscious that can really appreciate the flavor and texture of chocolate, and then place it in your mouth and lose yourself in the experience.

Another chapter talks about having the right state out when you enjoy sex. Sex can be hum drum or horrific, even with someone you love, if you have the wrong Resource State out, but it can be wonderful if you have a Resource State out that feels safe, sensual, and lost in the experience.

To be present in each moment and to have the best Resource State out our states need to be in a Normal condition (see chapters 5, 6 and 7). Our states are our tools, our resources. Just as the master carpenter knows which tool to use each time, we can learn our states and select the best one to finish our work and to enjoy our living.

With practice, you will become able to notice how you are experiencing something and to assess if you have the right Resource State out. For example, if you are driving through a beautiful mountainous area while thinking about the issues at work the experience of the drive is being wasted. If this happens you can give a message to the state that is concerned about the issues at work that you will give it some time later in the day to focus on what needs to be decided, and you can let that state know that you want to be able to enjoy this drive. Then, you can invite out a Resource State that can really enjoy the colors, distances, and beauty of the drive.

When you invite a state out to enjoy something, whether it is a beautiful drive, a piece of chocolate, or a hot bath it usually results in the right Resource State quickly being available. It is already there waiting, wanting to be out to enjoy what it is really good at enjoying. Resource States want to help. They want to do what they are the best state to do. Given the opportunity, they are eager to come out and enjoy.

What sometimes blocks enjoyment

Vaded, Retro, and Conflicted states can interfere with our enjoyment. If our right-hand is feeling pain it is difficult to enjoy the left hand getting a massage. If the right-hand is pain-free we may really be able to focus on the massage. This is the key to enjoyment.

You can call it good mental health or you can call it 'all Resource States being in a Normal condition', but this is what is needed. This allows the permission for enjoyment.

One way to achieve good mental health is to focus on how easy it is to enjoy the things that you are doing. By seeing if we can really truly enjoy where we are, we can see if we still have some work to do in moving states to Normalcy.

If you find that you cannot enjoy the things that you are doing then you have Resource States that are blocking the enjoyment. You have Resource States that can benefit from moving from where they are to a state of normalcy.

For example, if you want to enjoy a piece of chocolate and you have a Resource State that is screaming at you from the inside, "Don't eat that," then you will not really be able to enjoy it as well as you would if all Resource States were happy for you to have it. You have Conflicted states. You have a state that wants to eat the chocolate, and you have a state that is telling you not to eat it. These Resource States will need to learn to appreciate each other, to internally communicate, and compromise so that you will be able to eat an amount of chocolate that all states feel good about, an amount of chocolate that you can truly enjoy.

If you want to enjoy sitting in a hot tub with warm churning water moving around your skin in a relaxing way, you will not be able to do this if you have a Resource State that is afraid of water and afraid of being in the tub. Your experience might be one of panic rather than enjoyment. This is a Vaded state coming out with its feelings of fear into a situation where those feelings do not really fit. This Vaded state will need to get the nurturance, understanding, love, and the support that it needs so it can feel comfortable resting back in the background. When this happens your more mature and sensual states can enjoy the experience of a hot tub, freely.

If you have an opportunity to visit your sister after a number of years and you find yourself unable to communicate, feeling like you did when you were small and at home you may have a Retro state that is responding to her in the way that it learned when you were a child. That way of responding to her when you were a child may have been the best way for you to survive then, but it may not be the way you want to respond to her now, or the way that you can really enjoy being with her.

In order to really be able to enjoy the visit with your sister you may need to attend to your Retro state (Chapter 7), making sure it has a role that works for you today, so your Resource State that can really enjoy your sister can have permission to be out.

Life is to be savored, not tolerated

Learn to accept nothing less than enjoying living. There will obviously be times when you do things that you do not find enjoyable. Getting a tooth drilled may not be enjoyable, but it is something that you wisely choose to do. There may be work that needs to be done that you do not find enjoyable. Even at these times there may be better Resource States to be out, so the experience is the best it can be, even though it may not be enjoyed. But there are many times in life that we can truly enjoy what we are experiencing. It is a waste to accept anything less than enjoying these times.

A few years ago I was in Fiji for a holiday. There were a lot of people there who are not wealthy. I saw houses at night where light came out of the walls between almost every board, but I was impressed by how happy many of the people were. They laughed, waved, kidded, and appeared to really enjoy living. It was not money that helped them enjoy living.

The day after I returned home I was in a large supermarket stocking up on some of the things that I needed. I was struck while looking around at the other shoppers at the lack of enjoyment I saw. People were busy, focused, and they did not look like they were having a very good time. There were almost no smiles, little lightness, and little enjoyment. I felt I had moved from a place where there was more lightness, laughter and enjoyment to a place where there was more concern about keeping up with the duties of life.

It is good to think about what we want, not what we should do or what we have to do. We have parts in us that want to do things, that will enjoy doing things, and that may want a toy of some form. We need to practise letting those Resource States out. We need to practice freeing them so we can enjoy.

When Vaded states are resolved that frees them to be able to do the roles that they used to do. If my playful Resource State experienced a trauma and held onto the trauma it can again be playful once it gets a resolution with the help and support from other states. Therefore, by achieving a higher level of mental health we have more states free to us to enjoy living.

When we take away the competition, the need to impress, any fear, any sense of not being good enough, we are left with a feeling of being free to be who we are. We are left with an ability to choose what we want to do to have fun, with an ability to say what we want to say to engage, with an ability to be in the moment and respond immediately and freely. When we do not fear the moment we can live the moment.

> **Being psychologically healthy means we can live in a way that when we come to the end we can be happy when we look back.**

Imagine being with someone who is talking about how big their car is, how important their job is, about the designer clothes that they have purchased, someone who is trying to impress. One way of responding to the person would be to try to compete by saying what you have. That conversation is not one of lightness. A better thing to do might be to talk about things you both find enjoyable, or to just get away from that person.

A good thing to ask yourself is what you would enjoy to talk about with this person. What is it about this person that you would like to know, that you would find interesting. You can completely ignore this person's trying to build themselves up and ask them whatever you would like to ask them. You might wonder about their kids, about their views on life, about the last place they travelled where they had fun. You might find something to talk with this person about that you could enjoy. You might have fun and enjoy the conversation. This is what can happen when your Resource States are Normal and don't have a need to compete.

Healthy people are not selfish. They enjoy connecting with others and they enjoy helping others see the top half of the glass. They may find they enjoy giving more than receiving. Being psychologically healthy means we can live in a way that when we come to the end we can be happy when we look back.

Chapter 23: Other than Resource States what else is inside?

This book is about Resource States, but that is not all we have inside of us. It is fascinating what I and others have observed in working with hypnosis and Resource States.

Several years ago I wrote an article about what lies within. In it, I mentioned five things:

- Resource States,
- Introjects,
- Inner self,
- Create a form identities (CFIs), and
- Other personalized introjects (OPIs).

I will tell about each of them in this chapter.

Resource States

In psychology, there has long been a debate about what is nature and what is nurture, what is heredity and what is environment. It was explained at the beginning of this book that our Resource States come from training, from our living, from our nurture. While how we are born, our nature, impacts upon the types of Resource States we develop, all Resource States are developed as a result of our life situations. We may be born naturally to be more bold, or less bold, more conservative or less conservative, and that will impact on the types of Resource States we develop.

When we do something over and over again as a coping mechanism to a life situation we grow a neural bundle of fibres, a neural pathway and that is a Resource State. We use these Resource States that we grow in a way that best suits us. So, our Resource States are parts of our brain, physiological, and have been created by the way that we have coped with life situations. Resource States have their own special traits.

Resource State traits
- They are created by repetition usually in childhood.
- They are a physiological part of the brain.
- They cannot be destroyed and they cannot leave.
- They can slightly change their role, and they can change the amount they come out.
- They are our inner resources.
- We can feel an inner peace when they respect each other and get along.
- They can be vaded when they carry unresolved issues from the past.
- They can be Retro when they continue with a role that no longer suits us.
- They can be Conflicted when they do not respect other Resource States.
- They can be Normal when they are relaxed and they help us externally and get along internally.

Introjects

Introjects are fairly easy to understand. They are our internalized impressions of other people. We have Introjects of everyone we know, and even everyone we imagine. If we know someone or can imagine a person we can play act that person just like an actor in a movie pretends to be someone else.

An interesting thing about Introjects is that each one of our Resource States has its very own Introjects of other people. This is why you may find yourself liking someone in one Resource State and not liking that same person while you are in another Resource State. For example, you may have a Resource State that is fragile and needs love. This Resource State may really want a relationship with someone who gives it love. But another Resource State that is more intellectual may not have respect for that other person because they are not challenging.

While you are in one Resource State you may feel, "I love you," and while in the other Resource State you may feel like you really have to get out of this relationship. Each of the two Resource States have their own different Introject for the same other person.

An abusive father may be loved by one Resource State and may be detested by the Resource State that has been abused by him. Here again the two Resource States have different Introjects for the same person, the father.

It is our Resource States that introject Introjects. In other words, each of our Resource States forms an internal impression of another person, and introjects the person into its memory.

We can have an Introject that we fear internally. This fear is really an illusionary fear because Introjects are not really real in a sense of something that can hurt us, other than the power that we give them inside. A real person can hit us and can hurt us, but an Introject of that person is just an internalized impression that we hold on the inside. It has no real power, other than the power we give it. The techniques in Chapter 5 to heal Vaded Resource States are to help Resource States that have held fear of Introjects to release their fear and feel supported, to learn that there is nothing really there on the inside that can hurt. Sharing an internal unconditional loving and understanding hug from that charged helper, right hand, is a way they can learn the fearful introject is past, over, obsolete and their internal space can be clear and free.

Our Resource States have Introjects of inspiring people, of people we love, of people we would like to be more like, and the people who we dislike and sometimes fear.

Probably none of our Introjects are entirely accurate. This makes sense because each of our Resource States holds different impressions of different people. It is obvious that they cannot all be right. It is probable that none of them are completely right. Therefore, our Introjects do not really represent another person completely and accurately. That is okay. They still serve us well. We learn from them, we can love them, and we can be inspired by them.

We may learn from an Introject that the person who is has been Introjected should be avoided. That can be a good thing to learn. If someone is dangerous it is probably wise to avoid them.

But it is not wise to hold an internal fear that interferes with our day. The Resource State that holds an internal fear of an Introject is vaded. We have learned that there is no reason for a Resource State to hold an internal fear, although it is useful for a Resource State to hold an understanding that a person may be dangerous, so that person can be avoided in life.

Any power that an Introject has in us was internally given to it by the Resource State that introjected it, that holds it internally. That is pretty exciting because Resource States have the ability to learn. We have seen how Resource States can learn that their inner space can be safe and supported. This means they have learned that any introject that was internally feared can shrink and be sent away with the unconditional help of 'Helper' and the charged right hand, that shares acceptance and understanding love. And the Resource State that had in the past feared an introject can be given loving support by the nurturing state.

An intellectual Resource State may understand that Introjects are powerless, but a Vaded Resource State may still hold a fear of an Introject. That is why it is important for the Vaded state to be out when it learns empowerment and support. That is why the helping Resource State introduced in Chapter 5 needs to be ready to be supportive when a Vaded Resource State comes to the surface.

While I said that Introjects are internalized impressions of other people, we can also have Introjects of things that are not people. Obviously, we can have Introjects of our pets. We can even have Introjects of things like a storm. It is possible to hold a fear of a storm on the inside that has been introjected. We can also have an introject of a beautiful stream.

Resource States may be vaded by Introjects of things that are not people. For example, a Resource State may hold an internalized fear of a wild animal, a storm, or anything else that has been introjected. While it is wise to hold an understanding that something may need to be avoided on the outside, it is not good to continue to fear something on the inside.

It is not good to empower something on the inside that we do not want to empower, or that does not deserve to be empowered. It is appropriate to reclaim our internal power and for all of our Resource States to learn that the inside is a place of peace and safety, even if the outside may sometimes not be.

It is possible for a Resource State to decide that it no longer wants an Introject in its space. For example, if a person has been involved in a gunpoint robbery the Resource State that was out during the robbery will hold an introject of the robber. This state may hold an internalized fear of the robber. A more intellectual Resource State may see the robber as someone who is troubled and needs help.

It is possible for the Resource State that holds the fear of the robber to gain an understanding that the introjected robber on the inside has no power. This fantasized introject can be spoken to on the inside of the psyche by a Resource State that has been afraid of him. This fantasized introject can be told anything the fearful Resource State chooses to say.

This could be done by the fearful Resource State imagining the robber in another chair across the room, while at the same time knowing that he is not really there. By imagining the robber in that chair the fearful Resource State can say everything that would have been unsafe or inappropriate to say during the robbery.

This expression by the fearful Resource State allows that Resource State to better understand that the Introject has no power on the inside. Understanding this, that the Introject has no power inside, allows the fearful Resource State to tell the Introject, "I do not want you in my inner space. Get out now." In this way the Resource State that was fearful, was vaded, re-claims its power and is no longer vaded.

Introject traits

- Introjects are created by a Resource State taking on an internalized impression.
- Each Resource State will have its own Introjects, so one Resource State may like a person and another Resource State may not like that same person. One Resource State may see a person as loving and another Resource State may see that same person as boring.
- Resource States may hold any emotion about an Introject. For example, a Resource State may love, respect, fear, or hate an Introject.
- A Vaded Resource State is vaded because of the impressions it holds about Introjects.
- A Resource State can learn that Introjects are merely internalized impressions and that they have no real power on the inside.

- Introjects may be asked to leave by a Resource State once the Resource State realizes the Introject is powerless.
- Because Introjects are merely internalized impressions they are not necessarily accurate representations. What is perceived about a person may or may not be accurate.
- Resource States may be empowered by positive Introjects, inspired by them, and can learn from them.
- It is possible for a Resource State to think about what an admired Introject would do to get inspiration in how to handle situations in life.

Inner self

Inner self is a part that has different traits tha Resource States. It is the one part that everyone seems to have, and unlike Resource States it reports having always been here.

Until now this chapter has been about the physiological, the Resource States that are a natural physical part of the brain and Introjects which are memories Resource States hold of other people. Inner self is a part that is a bit different. Inner self can appear to have access to information around the beginning of life or around the end of life.

Many of you will have heard of near-death experiences (NDE). A lot has been written about these experiences by Elizabeth Kubler-Ross and others. Some people, at a time when they had been deemed clinically dead, having no heartbeat and no electrical brain activity, have reported that they were able to observe what was occurring to their body, often from the vantage point of floating above the body. Some of these people report moving from their body to another room in the hospital or across the country, and they have been able to report accurate observations about what they had seen. Some people who have been blind since birth report accurately what they have seen visually during their NDE.

What is this conscious awareness that can report information separate from the physical body? I call this part the Inner Self part. Some people call it higher self, inner strength, or spiritual self. I have found that hypnotized people can often accurately describe aspects of their birth even when their parents have no memory of having told them. They can then go back to their often surprised parents and get confirmation about things that happened during their birth. This, again seems possible because of the part I call Inner Self.

Inner Self reports being a part that we are born with, unlike Resource States that develop over time when the same coping mechanism is used again and again. When I speak directly with the Inner Self part of the client it always speaks with a clear, fearless voice and reports having some knowledge about what the person is here to learn. It will sometimes report being a central part of the person, and it will sometimes report that it is rarely accessed. I do not see inner self as a Resource State. I sometimes access this part intentionally if the client presents with an issue of needing direction in life.

Inner self traits
- It reports having always been with the client.
- It is the one state that everyone appears to have.
- It speaks with a clear, strong, caring voice.
- It claims to have wisdom about the purpose of the person.

- It sometimes reports wishing it was listened to more.
- It can have a low level of energy or a higher level of energy.

Other personalized introjects (OPIs)

OPIs are very interesting. There is no doubt that they exist and that they are observable, especially when working with hypnosis. There is doubt about what they are. In this section I will tell about their traits, when they come out, and how I have worked with them. I find them to be quite rare. In order to draw a better picture of OPIs I will describe how they are observed during therapy, when using hypnosis.

During hypnosis when, as a therapist, I am talking directly with Resource States, the Resource States will claim to be a part of the person. Normal Introjects are merely internalized impressions of someone else. As I stated above, each Resource State will have its own Introjects. You can only access an Introject via a Resource State, because an Introject is a Resource State's impression of another person.

While a client is hypnotized, if I were to ask to speak to an Introject of the client's mother there could be an inner confusion about which Introject I wanted to talk with. It might be the mother of the surface Resource State that spoke with the mother earlier in the same day, or it might be the mother introject of the child Resource State and this child Resource State may hold very different memories and opinions of mother. So it is clear that Introjects are not part of the person other than being an internalized impression held by individual Resource States.

OPIs are very different from Resource States, inner self, and Normal Introjects. While everyone has Resource States, an inner self state, and Introjects not everyone has OPIs. Like Normal Introjects, OPIs appear not to be a Resource State part of the person, but unlike Normal Introjects a single OPI can relate to many different Resource States and be seen by them in the same way. Therefore, it is clear that an OPI is not an impression held by a single Resource State. OPIs have a single identity across all the Resource States that know them.

When an OPI is asked, "Are you part of this person?" it will respond with something like, "No, I'm not part of her." OPIs speak about the client in the third person, "She will never amount to anything." While some Resource States will speak about other Resource States in the third person, "I don't like that part," there is normally an acknowledgment that the two Resource States are different parts of the same person. When talking with an OPI there is an impression that you are almost talking with someone else, and not the client.

OPIs will often say things like, "I know I shouldn't be here." "You can't make me leave," or "I am afraid to go." Sometimes OPIs will even claim to be another person who has died.

OPIs appear to be detrimental for the client. Regardless of how we interpret what an OPI is, I find that it is most therapeutic to help the OPI to leave. This is not possible with a Resource State, as a Resource State is a physical part of the body, made of trained axon and dendrite synaptic connections.

There is a cross-cultural conception that there is a place of light where loved ones are waiting. This belief crosses many religions and ideologies. I, therefore, use the image of a place of light to negotiate with OPIs to leave and go to this better place, and after this has happened, almost without exception, the client will report feeling lighter and more free.

Often the client will report that the very critical voice that may have been heard for years is no longer heard. After an OPI has been negotiated with to leave I have never had the client come back to me and say that they wish it was there again. When an OPI leaves, following the negotiation, there is a very positive and good feeling. There is real therapeutic value.

There is a fundamental difference between an OPI and a Resource State. A Resource State is a physiological part of the person and it cannot leave. It is part of the brain, a neural pathway. It is possible to ask a Resource State to leave and it may agree to do so, but the next time the client is hypnotized if you asked to talk to that Resource State, it is immediately there and able to talk. Therefore, it appears that Resource States do not leave, and cannot leave, but may sometimes step into the background. When an OPI leaves and later if you ask to speak with that OPI a Resource State will speak up and say something like, "He's not here. He left." It is very clear that OPIs can leave, and when they do they are no longer available for conversation.

OPIs could be looked at as an unknown manifestation of the dynamic brain. The personality is truly fascinating. OPIs will sometimes report reasons why they are there. They often will say, "Don't make me leave. I don't want to die." They occasionally report being a relative or friend of the person to whom I am talking. They sometimes report the sense of being lost, and they sometimes report that they are needed to be with this person, often to be critical of them, 'to keep them in line'. They sometimes share the belief that if they go they will die, or that they can't go where they should, 'Into the light,' because they are not good enough to be there.

They are often, although not always, negative and they often express being confused. They are sometimes gruff and highly critical. Very occasionally they can appear malevolent.

Over the years I have developed techniques for negotiating with OPIs so the client can feel lighter and relieved. I have found it does not matter what the client thinks about OPIs, and I do not try to convince the client to think about them in any way. After the therapy, I merely ask, "How are you feeling now?" and how the client reports this is what is important to me.

Here is how I negotiate with OPIs to leave. As stated above, there appears to be an archetypal impression of going to a white light where there are loved ones waiting, where there is an unconditional love, and where there is peace. Interestingly, when I ask an OPI how they feel about going to the white light I have never gotten a question, "What is that?" There has been an implicit understanding of the white light as being a place where some people go. This underlines the cross-cultural acceptance of this archetype.

First, I establish that I am speaking with an OPI, that is, a part that says that it is not part of the person, a part that sees the person as someone else, and a part that recognizes that it is not where it should be.

OPIs are often nervous about speaking with me, because they are afraid I will make them go someplace else and they are afraid of what that might be like. Therefore, I tell the OPI that I am not going to make them do anything. I tell them that anything that they do is going to be totally up to them, and I also say that I know that it seems like you are not able to go to the light, but that you will be able to if you want to. They often at first have difficulty accepting this.

OPIs generally see themselves as 'not good enough' to go to the light. They think they would not be welcome there, and that they would not fit in. Therefore, I tell them that it is true that they cannot take their negativity with them, they cannot take their dark heavy anger and resentment and jealousy with them but that they can go to the light. I tell them that we can do an experiment so they can see, then if they want everything back like it was they can have it that way. I have found it is important that they not feel pushed or coerced.

I tell them that there is a magical sieve that we will use. I tell them that only the part of them that can go to the light will be able to pass through the sieve and that the sieve will collect all the negativity, all the dark sticky, heavy bits and it is totally impossible for that stuff to go through the sieve. I tell them that the sieve is much more powerful than it needs to be so passing through will be like taking off a heavy coat and leaving it in the sieve.

I tell them that they can now allow themselves to fall straight through the sieve and feel what it is like to be only the part of them that can go to the light. I then ask them to look back up at the sieve and tell me what that stuff in the sieve looks like. They normally say it is dark and heavy and they often say it looks sticky. I then ask them, "Do you want any of that back?" They always say that they do not want anything back from the sieve. They are emphatic about that.

I then ask what color of light or fluid would sizzle that stuff in the sieve into nothingness. When they tell me a color I then ask, "Is that a light or is that a fluid." When they tell me, then I say let's just have that, for example, purple light sizzle straight through the sieve and sizzle that stuff into complete nothingness, and I make a sizzling noise.

Then I say something like, "Now, there is someone who loves you that is pulling you like a magnet to come to the light to where they are waiting." I tell them to just allow yourself to feel the pull and to go on and see what it is like there in the light. I tell them to just go for a visit and see what they want to do. I tell them to just allow themselves to be drawn into that complete unconditional love by that magnetic pull.

At about this time an interesting thing happens to the ambiance of the room. Where there had been a sense of trepidation and fear, the room fills with a sense of lightness. The voice of the OPI becomes very soft, relaxed and even sometimes euphoric. I then tell the OPI that it can stay there where the light is if it wants to, and I ask it if that is what it would like to do. It is very happy to stay. I tell it that is fine and tell it that it is good that it will be able to enjoy where it now is.

I pause for a few seconds, and then I address the client directly by name, and ask something like, "How are you feeling now?" Practically without exception, the client reports feeling physically lighter.

This work feels like some of the best work I do. Before I started working in this way with clients who manifested this negative, "I am not part of her" part, these clients were very slow to progress and then it was often limited progress. Following up with clients after their OPI leaves, I have received feedback from, "I have not really noticed much difference," to, "My whole life has changed. The loud critical voice on the inside is no longer there and I feel so much better, lighter and more able to be myself."

For those who might be interested, here are some examples of what OPI's have said in relation to how they got where they were. Please interpret them in a way that works for you.

> When Mary was a little girl we shared the same hospital room. My body died and I did not want to die so I came with Mary. I know I shouldn't have. (This OPI needed assurance that going to the light was just moving to a place of love where someone was waiting, and it was not dying.)
>
> I am her (the client's) mother. I have to be here to keep her in line. If I was not here she would make too many mistakes. (This OPI was experienced as a loud critical voice on the inside.)
>
> You can't make me go because her (dead) husband would be angry with me for me being here for so long. (With negotiation, this OPI was convinced that anger would not be a problem in the light, and was convinced to

go close enough to the light as an experiment so he could see this clearly. Afterward, he was happy to go on.)

I can't go to the light, because I am blind. (This OPI reported being blinded when a shell when off in a battle. I asked him to just reach out with his hand and see if someone who loved him would take it and help him. With an immediate mood change he reported someone did.)

I can't leave here. I don't belong there. (This is a common thing for OPIs to say. It is quite easy for them to understand they do belong there, although the dark negativity they have held onto does not belong there. At first they may be extremely adamant that they can't or won't go, but they can quickly change in this when it is made clear to them that their real core, them, can go, just not with the negative coat, not with their negative feelings. This is when I sometimes tell them that it is like taking off a heavy coat and I give them the image of passing through the sieve to separate themselves from the negativity.)

> **The brain is an amazing thing and it is difficult or impossible to interpret the different things that are manifested in the personality.**

I have found that almost all OPIs report being there because they fear moving on, or do not believe there is a place for them to move on to. Sometimes they report being there to "Keep her in line." In the more rare instances of OPIs reporting that they do not want to leave a loved one, I tell them than they can go to the light and then still guide them from the light. I tell them that it is their being stuck that causes the client to feel heavy. Being free to move to the light does not mean a separation. I tell them that the loving connection can be stronger when there is no fear. They are then able to leave.

Traits of OPIs

- They report that they are not part of the person.
- The same OPI can be seen as the same by a number of different Resource States, unlike introjects that are interpreted differently by each Resource State. Each Resource State has its own introjects.
- They report that they are not where they should be.
- They usually report feeling unable to move to where they should be.
- They are often a very critical voice inside the person. (It is also possible for a Resource State to be a critical voice.)
- When it is made clear that they can move to where they should be, but they just cannot take negativity with them, they change in their resistance.
- They can leave and afterward Resource States continue to report that they are no longer present.
- When they move to 'where the light is' they become euphoric and happy to stay with the light, and this leaves the person feeling physically lighter and with a sense of being more free to be themselves.

The brain is an amazing thing and it is impossible to interpret all the different things that are manifested in the personality.

Philosophically, an interesting aspect about working with OPIs is how what they say seems to align with much religious teaching. Many religions teach that one needs to live a life of love to be able to go to heaven or to move forward to what lies next. Most often OPIs report not feeling like they can go to the light because they do not feel they belong there, because of the negativity they hold. This aligns with the teaching of, "Live a good life to go to the loving here-after." There seems to be a cross-cultural, cross-religious agreement about this, and this is manifested in the nature of the OPI.

Creative form identities (CFIs)

Creative form identities are merely a creative way for Resource States to be represented. These may happen spontaneously or they may be created. In Chapter 5 of this book, that pertains to healing the Vaded state, one of the steps in the process is to embody a healing, nurturing Resource State into a helping hand so that hand can be used to assist in the healing of a fragile Resource State that feels a need for nurturance. This, embodiment of a Resource State into a hand, is a creative form identity, a CFI.

I once had a client who was bingeing and who was concerned about his big stomach, as well as his health. Using hypnosis I asked to speak to a Resource State that either had some knowledge of the bingeing or was the Resource State that was responsible for the bingeing. I ask that Resource State when it was ready to speak to say, "I'm here." After a small pause I heard a faint, "I'm here."

I thanked the state for speaking to me and asked it if it knew something about the bingeing, or if it caused the bingeing. It replied, "Yes, I do that." I asked again if it was the part that actually caused the bingeing and it replied that it was.

I asked this Resource State, "What name or term fits you? What can I call you?" It replied that I could call it, "Fishy." I commented that that is an interesting name and ask why it wanted me to call it Fishy. It replied that it wanted to be called Fishy because, "I am a fish." I said, "Oh you are. That is interesting. I really want to hear about why you cause the bingeing."

This Resource State that saw itself as a fish told me that it caused the bingeing because it was lonely and that it needed a friend. It said that if it had more room to swim around it might be able to find a friend. It had decided that if the stomach grew bigger it would have a better chance of finding a friend, and then it would not be lonely. It was a Vaded Resource State that held onto the feelings of loneliness.

The mind is an amazing and dynamic thing. I am often awe struck by how amazing and dynamic it is. This Resource State had learned to identify itself as a fish, possibly because of some fascination with fish as a child, and it was lonely. It is not unusual for Resource States to have needs, like the need for friendship, the need for love, and the need to feel protected.

This Fishy Resource State needed a friend. It was somewhat unusual in that it identified itself as a fish. This is an example of a CFI. It was a Resource State that had developed a creative form identity for itself.

To finish the story about Fishy, I asked him if I were to find him a friend who could play with him if he would stop causing the bingeing. He said, "I guess that would be okay." I then ask to speak with another part who liked to play, and who would enjoy playing with a fish in a nice way. I ask that part to say, "I'm here." A Resource State spoke up and I negotiated the two to be friends and to stay together on the inside. Fishy was happy and the client reported that after the session he stopped bingeing.

Sometimes Resource States are represented as a tightness in the stomach or some other physiological feeling in some part of the body. Sometimes they are represented as the left hand or the right hand. It is not unusual for a person to notice a different psychological feeling on one side or in one part of the body than they feel on the other side or in another part of the body. These are all CFI representations of Resource States.

A CFI is merely a Resource State that is either temporarily or permanently represented in some other form. It recognizes that it is part of the person and in all other ways it is like a Resource State other than its representation in a creative form.

It is sometimes the case that a CFI will see itself as another person. This more often happens if the traits of the Resource State match closely with the traits of the other person, for example a Resource State that shares a lot of traits with 'dad' may say it is 'dad'. This is just another type of creative form identification. The CFI dad is not an Introject, as it is not Resource State specific (different for every Resource State), and it is not a OPI in that it knows it is part of the person and is where it belongs. These 'other person' CFIs are often manifested in people suffering from Multiple Personality (DID), but they also occasionally appear in other clients.

Traits of CFI's

- They see themselves as part of the person.
- They identify themselves as a part of the body or as some other creative form.
- They are Resource States and are like Resource States in all ways other than their self-identification.
- They have the same kinds of needs that Resource States have and respond in the same way to Resource State interventions.
- They sometimes maintain their creative form identity only temporarily before taking on a normal identity, and they sometimes maintain a creative form identity without taking on a normal identity.

When I speak about a Normal identity for a Resource State I am talking about the Resource State seeing itself as a person of a certain age. A Resource State may see itself as a five-year-old, it may see itself as the age of the person, and occasionally it may see itself as older than the person. Normally Resource States that see themselves as older than the person do this because they feel tired and rundown. They feel older, therefore they see themselves as older. OPIs, which as we learned above are not Resource States, also often report themselves as being older than the person.

When a Resource State sees itself as older than the person, or when a Resource State sees itself as the opposite sex from the person it could be considered a CFI.

It is not unusual for Resource States to see themselves as the opposite sex of the person. This usually happens when the traits of a Resource State match the stereotype of the gender. For example, a female who has a Resource State that is very bold and aggressive may see this Resource State as male, and the male who has a Resource State that is intuitive or nurturing may identify the state as female. It is more common for individuals to see all of their Resource States as the same gender that they are, but there is no problem if individuals have Resource States that identify themselves as the opposite sex of the person.

What lies within

The answer to the question, "What lies within?" is there are five internal identities:

- Resource States: physiological parts of the brain that are neural pathways that have been trained over time to have a certain level of emotion and intellect, and to supply us with a certain role.
- Introjects: internalized impressions of other people or other things that each Resource State holds. Each Resource State will have its own impression of individuals, animals and events.
- Inner strength: the one part that we all have. This appears to be the part that we are born with and that we die with. It is a part that reports near-death experiences, can

report birth experiences, and it claims to have an awareness of life purpose.
- OPIs: these report not being part of the person and they may be negotiated with to leave. They normally interfere with the person's ability to feel in control of their life.
- CFI's: these are Resource States that have taken on a creative form in the way they identify themselves. Other than the creative form identity they are Resource States in every other way.

We are dynamic beings. I am constantly amazed at how we are put together and how we can change. It is empowering to be aware of what is going on inside us. Understanding our resources allows us the opportunity to use them. Healing Vaded states, improving our inner Resource State relationships, and learning how each state can help us allows us to know and be ourselves.

Chapter 24: Growth and being ready for it

This book is about becoming free to be who we really are. This means that we are not held back from being who we are by random emotion, by inner conflict, by inner fears, or by a reluctance to change.

There may be a part of us that knows and understands how we really want to be but there may be other parts that are used to the old, and have difficulty accepting the new.

Change can happen quickly when we get the different parts of ourselves to agree on what we want. It takes courage to decide we are ready to change and commitment to step over the line, but big change happens when the parts of us that had been obstacles can come on side.

I believe that change or growth comes in stages. We cannot move from one stage or level until we finish the last, or have at least made real progress on it.

Hurdle levels for growth

Here are the 5 hurdles for growth.

Intent: We have to want to grow before change can happen.

Wisdom: Once we have a positive intention to grow our minds will become open to how this growth can occur. Holding the positive intention to grow brings the wisdom that is needed to grow.

> **Honesty exposes our feelings.**

Courage: Once we know what we need to do it takes courage to actually do it. It takes courage to change. We have to have the motivation and the effort to move from where we were to where we want to be.

Honesty: Honesty is an important step. Unless we can be honest with ourselves and others we cannot get a picture of how we are doing in our growth. We cannot know where we are. Everything is fuzzy. Everything is confused. Honesty is a great clarifier. We cannot know if someone accepts us, likes us, or loves us unless we are honest. If someone says to you, "I love you," and you have been honest with them then you know they love you. But, if you have not been honest with them you cannot be sure if they love you, or love only what you pretend to be. Dishonesty covers life in a fog.

Love: When we are true to ourselves and to others we have a direct route from soul to soul. Our honesty exposes our feelings. We have an opportunity to feel love toward others, and to feel love from others.

Transcendence: The final step in growth is transcendence. This is our ability to love everything and every person. This is the ability to have understanding and acceptance of those who are still growing. It is a tall order but a good vision.

Growth and our parts

Growth and our parts are tied closely together. Our psyche is our tool for change. We cannot move forward in growth if we have parts that are carrying trauma and no resolution from the past. Injured states have too much fear or feelings of rejection to allow us to move forward with growth.

If we have conflicted states it is difficult to focus on growth. If we have conflicted states we focus on the battle inside us rather than on the vision of the growth we want to make.

In order for us to be ready to follow the steps for growth our parts need to be healed and at peace.

Example of growth: Tammie

Tammie has not been able to be in a relationship with a man where she can feel connected, loved, and where she can feel that she loves him for an extended period of time. She has had dreams of a good relationship, she has had positive urges for a good relationship, but she has never really been able to feel connected in a relationship in an ongoing basis. At first, she thought she just was not finding the right guy, but over the years she had to accept that there must be something about her that keeps her from finding the relationship that she wants.

Intent

Intent is the first hurdle requirement for change.

The race car driver that wrecks every car may need to change his driving style.

Before Tammie can have a chance to get what she wants she has to have an intent to change. That means she has to accept that there is something about her that needs changing and she has to be ready to focus energy on making that change happen. She has to want it. When she does this she will be able to say to herself, "I want to do whatever it takes within myself so I can be open for the kind of relationship that I want."

This intent to change opens a door for that change to be able to happen for Tammie. If she were just to continue to blame each guy she meets and continue to look for 'Mr Right' she would probably spend the rest of her life feeling that she was just unlucky in love.

The race car driver that wrecks every car may need to change his driving style more than just his cars. It would be frustrating to an observer watching the driver wreck car after car, then hearing the driver complain about how bad the cars were. In the same way, although they may not say it, Tammie's friends may be frustrated at her continuing to blame each guy she meets as the cause for the failure in her relationships.

Tammie has gotten to the point in her life where she is ready to change. She has a positive intent to change something about herself so that she can have the kind of relationship that she wants.

Wisdom

As soon as she achieves intent she will start thinking, "What is it about me that is keeping me from having the kind of relationship I want?" The search for the answer is on. She will start noticing patterns in her relationships and she will start getting an idea about the kinds of things she may need to change in herself.

It is the uneasy struggle with intent that gives birth to wisdom. That does not mean that wisdom comes immediately, or that the first thoughts are the right ones.

When the hiker sets an intent to travel to the snow topped mountain the goal has been set. He or she would probably never get there without the clear intent. There can then be a continued movement toward the peak, even if occasionally the wrong path is taken. The more movement is made, the more wisdom there is about the final trail that will arrive there.

When Tammie thinks about what has happened in her relationships she realizes that each time she has started getting close in relationships she started noticing aspects of her partners that turn her against them. Now that she realises this she begins to understand that she has a fear of closeness, a fear of connectedness. It is when closeness comes that she runs. We run from our fears. The fog is clearing for Tammie and she is getting a sharper idea about what is happening. She is getting Wisdom.

> **We have to be willing to be rejected before we can feel accepted.**

Courage

Tammie's intent has led her to wisdom. Now she needs the courage to do something about it. What will she do? She could see a therapist. She could even read a book like this one to work on her issue. In order for change to happen she has to have the courage to work on it. If she just relaxes back into her old habit she will continue to repeat finding and losing relationships.

It takes courage to change. You have to step up and do it or it will not happen. You have to be prepared to face who you are and decide you want to move from that place to where you want to be, and it will not happen without an effort. It is courage that brings the effort.

Honesty

Whichever way Tammie decides to face her issue and work on it she will have to have honesty. If she denies what is happening, if she tells a different story than the true one, change goes further into the distance. Tammie has to tell her therapist, her friends, herself, whoever and everyone the way things really are. She needs to fess up. As Tammie is honest it becomes much more clear to her what her responsibilities are. If she steps back and says, "It is really their fault" then she will be losing the opportunity to focus on what she needs to change.

It will be helpful for Tammie to be honest with her new partners. If she tells them what has happened in her last relationships that will help them to know her better and it will help them give her feedback if the same thing starts happening again. The biggest thing about being honest with them is it will allow Tammie to know that if her new partner still wants her when she is honest, then it is really her who they like. This can allow her to feel more secure in the relationship, to know she is liked.

Often people who are not honest in relationships fear that, "If he really knew me he would not like me." How can we know we are liked or loved if we have not been honest with the person who we are with? We have to have the courage to be honest before we can feel accepted by others. That takes courage. We have to be willing to be rejected before we can feel accepted.

If Tammie reads this book, she may discover that when she feels fear or panic in a relationship a Vaded state is coming out. She could use the steps in Chapter 5 on healing the Vaded state to help her ease the panic when it comes up. That means she will be able to make up her own mind about the relationship, rather than just run from it feeling out of control.

If Tammie is able to bring peace to any Vaded states that she might have, if she is honest with her partner, if she shows her true self and is able to stick with the relationship then she may experience love.

> **A relationship may not be unconditional, but love is.**

Love

Some people think love is that rush of finding a new relationship that feeds the lonely hunger of separation. They feed that hunger until they are no longer lonely then they think the love is gone. The love is not gone. It was never there. Love does not pop in and out like a woodpecker. When you love someone it is usually for life. You may not want to be with them for life, but you will still probably love them. It is knowing them and accepting them, and appreciating their soul. It is caring about their happiness. It is not contingent on the things they do. It is unconditional. The relationship may not be unconditional, but love is.

Love can only come when there is honesty, because we can only be known when we are honest. Living in pretence is not really living. It is pretending to live. To lie to someone and see them accept you gives no benefit of feeling accepted. Being gut wrenchingly honest when you look someone in the eyes and then see them accept you and care for you is the birthplace of love.

To maintain honesty in a relationship requires living a life that can be told. To maintain honesty in a relationship requires thinking before acting, "Is this something I will be able to feel comfortable being honest about?" Living a life of congruence means acting in a way today that we will feel good about tomorrow. It means the state that is considering doing something today is communicating on the inside with the state that will live with the consequences tomorrow. These are both good states and they should be able to communicate and compromise.

Love is the payoff for living the life of congruence and honesty. Love of others and of self. It is amazing to love, and to feel loved. It is possible to love people who cannot love you or themselves because they are not yet at that level in their growth to live 'honesty and openness'.

Transcendence

This step is an elusive one. It is one that Tammie will only be ready for once she has learned to love others and to accept and love herself. She will probably only be able to see it as a goal when she has learned the honest openness of love.

Transcendence is loving everyone and everything. It is appreciating the shark, the mosquito, and the villain who each play their part in life. It is possible for a loving parent to love their child even if that child does evil things. There can be a deep sadness when evil things are done, both for the receiver and the doer.

Evil comes from a lack of connection

The evil doer is a person who has not learned how to love or how to be loved. This is a person who may be reactive against others because of a feeling of separateness. The evil doer has turned off the feelings of connection and empathy, and has 'given up' on being loved and connected.

> **Evil is the hail of a frozen heart.**

It is sad when someone gives up, when someone is so far away from the feeling of love and connection that they allow a cold detachment inside. It is from that cold detachment that things are done that hurt, and sometimes to hurt.

Think of a parent seeing their child having this cold detachment, and the sadness they would feel that their child is away from the experience of love. The loving parent will feel a sadness, but will still love their child.

We often have to protect ourselves and others from the evil doer. Evil doers can hurt and do harm. They may even have to be imprisoned. But there is a difference between protecting ourselves and others, and internally detaching ourselves from those who have been unable to feel love and feel lovable. To chill ourselves and say about them that they are evil and deserve bad things is us detaching, and it is missing the sadness of what it is for them to be where they are.

They need what we may not be able to get to them, an awareness that they can be loved and that they are a member of a community of loving and lovable people. They need to realize they are not the evil they have done, that deep inside all that protection and defence is the child that both wants and can have love. That is a very hard message for them to hear and believe. It may go against their whole life experience.

All of us who have not attained transcendence have some of the evil doer inside us. It takes a detachment to wish someone to fail, to want to 'get back' at someone, or to selfishly lie. It takes detachment to hold on to the negative and heavy feelings of resentment, blame, anger, or jealousy. It is a cold feeling outside of understanding and compassion, to blame those with less for their position in life. It takes detachment to be racist, ageist, sexist, nationalist, or homophobic. Real courage and love is accepting everyone, and having a sadness for those who have not found the connectedness of love.

I am not saying to take all the locks off the doors. It is wise to protect oneself, one's home, community or country from evil or from being taken advantage of. It is not a kindness to someone to let them take advantage of you. It is actually more kind to be assertive and protect yourself in the same way anyone should be protected. To let someone bully you is teaching the bully that there is a payoff for bullying, and that is not a good thing to teach.

Non-appropriate behavior should be met with assertiveness in a firm and understanding way.

It can be a guide to an appropriate response to think of yourself as the loving parent of the person. How would you see their actions, and how would you deal with them?

I believe it takes a detachment to remove oneself from the suffering of animals, or from the devastation of an ecosystem. It is easier to look the other way, and to do what is easy or what looks best for the pocket book, but down inside there is a pulling away from the connectedness of everything when the path without courage and love is taken.

To reach transcendence it takes intent, wisdom, courage, and love. Then the vision of transcendence comes into view. Transcendence still eludes me.

When Tammie reaches transcendence she will be engaging and fun, she will not be drawn into conversations that are negative about others, although she may comment on what she feels is right, and she will feel acceptance for everyone, even if she may not accept all of the things they do. She will feel positive about herself and care more about relationships than her status or her finances.

> **She will not be hungry for love because she is living it.**

For most she will be a joy to be around, open and honest and fun, but for some who have a need to feed off being critical of others she may be seen as boring or uninteresting. For those who are the farthest from love, those who feel disconnected and do not see an ability to be connected, Tammie may represent what they cannot have. She may even be the person they would most like to attack, but if they gave themselves time to feel her acceptance it would help move them from their sadness and disconnect.

Tammie will feel relaxed in her world, able to appreciate its beauty and the amazingness of the relationships around her. She will value her experience here, the sounds, sights, colors, touch and tastes, and the ability to know, relate to, and love others. She will not be hungry for love because she is living it, but she will be easy to love because she will be nonthreatening, non-critical, and unconditionally accepting of the value of those around her.

She will be able to feel sadness and loss along with love and appreciation. Her body will be more healthy with less stress and anxiety, although it will age and succumb to normal physical ailments. She will live a life of lightness, free of the heavy negativity of hanging onto anger and resentment.

She will not fear death but she will want to sap the most experience she can of living. She will see even the painful parts of living as opportunities for growth that should not be missed. At the end of her life she will have a sense of appreciation for being here and for the connectedness she has had with others, with animals and with nature. She will pass easily, and she will be missed.

Chapter 25: Putting it all together

Learning about Resource States and about what lies within raises interesting questions about the personality and about, 'Who am I?' These questions are philosophically interesting and the conclusions that we make concerning these questions may help direct us to live more empowered lives.

If I am all my Resource States, then no one part of me is the real me. The real me is all my Resource States, and at any time in my life, the real me is especially those Resource States I am choosing to use the most at that time. This notion of choice is an important one, because if we have choice we can decide which Resource States will be out, we can decide how we want to experience living.

For thousands of years there has been debate on whether we can choose anything; whether our choices are predetermined like dominoes falling, or whether our choices are of our own choosing. Today, philosophers, scientists, physicists, and theologians have failed to agree on whether or not we have choice. Deep and dense arguments have been forwarded in an attempt to answer this question.

Sam Harris, a neuroscientist and philosopher, believes there is no such thing as free will. He calls it a non-starter, that there is no way the universe can be understood with the concept of free will. Yet he also says,

"If in fact we can't choose what we choose, how can choice be important? Why not just sit back and see what happens, why choose to do anything? Why get out of bed in the morning? Well, to choose to do nothing is itself a choice. And it is a very hard thing to do. You just sit there and wait to see what happens, and you are going to get impatient, you are going to get restless. You are going to be moved by impulses that you are going to have to choose to resist in order to just sit and wait and see what happens" (6:01, http://www.youtube.com/watch?v=iRIcbsRXQ0o).

It is somewhat difficult to accept his argument against freewill when he makes it by talking about the importance of the choices we make. Still, a poor argument does not mean the premise is wrong.

Michio Kaku, a theoretical physicist, believes we do have free will, because quantum physics reveals that there is uncertainty in what will come next. The universe is not just one of falling dominos. He argues that, because quantum physicists cannot know where an electron will show up next, there is uncertainty, hence we can have free will (http://www.youtube.com/watch?v=lFLR5vNKiSw). It seems as though knowing there is uncertainty in the universe provides for the possibility of free will, but does not necessarily prove it, but these are just two examples of the current debate over free will.

I believe we do have freewill, we do have a choice. I believe the fact that we fret back and forth over a decision is an indication that we have choice.

Whether you believe in evolution or divine creation nothing is here for no reason. There is a reason for everything that exists. We have two arms, we used two arms. We have two legs, we use two legs. We have a nose and we use our nose.

We do not have an extra arm dangling out of the middle of our back that we do not use. We fret and there must be a reason, a purpose for it. Fretting is not an errant manifestation that only a sick few do. We all fret. So, then, why do we fret? We spend a lot of time fretting.

> **We each have a lot of resources that we have built over our lifetimes.**

If our brains were merely evolved computers making the best decision for the moment it would be a straightforward, quick process of decision-making. That is not what happens. We go back and forth and back and forth in making many decisions. All that time would be wasted if it did not result in better decisions.

A predetermined decision does not need fretting time. A predetermined decision would take no more time than a straightforward weighing of options followed by a straightforward decision.

Because we spend time fretting, that time must be useful for something. Fretting cannot be a third arm in the middle of the back that is here for no use. It is useful, and it is used to allow us to make better decisions, therefore we do have decisions, and therefore we have choice in our lives.

Since we can choose, since we are not just carrying out the domino fall that started before we were born, we have the ability to become more who we choose to be.

It is exciting to know that we are not a single-minded person. It is exciting to know that we have several parts of us that we can choose from. We each have a lot of resources that we have built over our lifetimes, and we each have the ability to train the resources that we have to be different than they are.

If our Resource States have been trained over time to feel, to think, to synaptically fire in a certain way then we can continue to train them in the way we want them to be.

We can define how we want to be, which states we want to use, and how we want to train the states we have. We are a multiplicity of states and in this we have our freedom. We can be the masters of our own lives, and that is exciting.

It is not unusual to feel blocked in the ability to live an open and honest life that reflects the true self. When this happens we can heal our Vaded states, help our conflicted parts to compromise and respect each other, and we can learn to appreciate and use our inner resources so that we can be true to ourselves. It is important that we choose to live feeling empowered and at peace, being able to be real to ourselves and to others.

Fly Ride the Storm

Fly ride the melodic storm of life.
Feel the forceful winds and be proud of them,
for they are mutual to all who rise
to see the flash of light.
Choose stay above the cellar,
weathering the thunders of those who doubt.
Feel fear and woe and glad and glow,
for in these you have your freedom.
Fly ride the storm and fill you up
with winds that blow and bide you.
Your wings will grow and you may know
no place to hide inside you.

About the author:

Gordon Emmerson lives near Melbourne Australia. He is a psychologist and Resource State Therapist. His other books include, Ego State Therapy and Advanced Skills and Interventions in Therapeutic Counseling, and Resource Therapy Primer. He conducts Resource State Therapy and Ego State Therapy training workshops in Melbourne and around the world. Upcoming workshops can be found on http://www.egostatetherapy.com, or http://www.resourceherapy.com.

Made in the USA
Middletown, DE
30 July 2023